ten thousand

DEMOCRACIES

American Governance and Public Policy Series
Gerald W. Boychuck, Karen Mossberger, and Mark C. Rom, Editors

ten thousand
DEMOCRACIES

*Politics and Public Opinion in
America's School Districts*

Michael B. Berkman
Eric Plutzer

Georgetown University Press
Washington, D.C.

Georgetown University Press, Washington, D.C.
© 2005 by Georgetown University Press. All rights reserved.
Printed in the United States of America

10 9 8 7 6 5 4 3 2 1   2005

Portions of chapter 3 and 7, including some tabular matter, first appeared in Eric Plutzer's article "The Graying of America and Support for Funding the Nation's Schools." *Public Opinion Quarterly* 69, no. 1 (2005): 66–86, and is reprinted by permission of Oxford University Press.

Portions of chapter 7 also appeared in Michael B. Berkman and Eric Plutzer, "Gray Peril or Loyal Support? The Effects of the Elderly on Educational Expenditures," *Social Science Quarterly* 85 (December 2004): 1178–92, and is reprinted by permission of Blackwell Publishing.

As of January 1, 2007, 13-digit ISBN numbers will replace the current 10-digit system.
Paperback: 1-58901-076-5

Library of Congress Cataloging-in-Publication Data

  Berkman, Michael B., 1960–
  Ten thousand democracies: politics and public opinion in America's school districts / Michael B. Berkman, Eric Plutzer.
      p.   cm. — (American governance and public policy series)
  Includes bibliographical references and index.
  ISBN 1-58901-076-0 (pbk. : alk. paper)
  1. School districts—United States.   2. Politics and education—United States.
3. Education—United States—Public opinion.   I. Plutzer, Eric.   II. Title.
III. American governance and public policy.
  LB2817.3.B47 2005
  379.73—dc22   2005009497

*Dedicated to Ben, Clara, and Isaac
and the State College Area Public Schools*

Contents

List of Tables and Figures

Figures

Preface

The essence of democracy is popular sovereignty—the people rule. In the United States, the people rule indirectly by electing officials who they believe will best represent their values, aspirations, and interests. Between elections, many citizens continue to transmit their preferences by contacting elected officials, voting on referenda or initiatives, joining groups that will lobby on their behalf, talking to their friends and neighbors to sway public opinion, and expressing their opinions to journalists, pollsters, and anyone else who might convey their views to elected office holders.

Although we do not expect elected officials to perfectly mirror the preferences of their constituents, a government that consistently ignores the preferences of citizens can hardly be called democratic. For any government—the federal government of the United States or of other nations, the various state governments, municipal governments, or school boards—we can ask how closely enacted public policies actually correspond to what the public prefers. The degree of correspondence is what political scientists refer to as *policy responsiveness*. In this book, we explore policy responsiveness in American school districts by looking at how much school boards spend on K–12 education and whether these spending policies comport with the preferences of the citizens who live in those districts.

Although topics come and go in political science, the study of policy responsiveness has been an exciting empirical enterprise for more than four decades. It remains a core concept because it lies at the intersection of so many different areas of study. For example, understanding and evaluating the relationship between what people want and what they get from government involves the study of public opinion. Indeed, one reason the study of policy responsiveness has been so lively is that it presents formidable methodological challenges in measuring people's attitudes and preferences. To meet these challenges, political scientists have found clever ways to use historical information (McDonagh 1992, 1993) and inventive and sophisticated methods to utilize demographic and survey data (Weber et al. 1972; Erikson, Wright, and McIver 1993; Erikson, MacKuen, and Stimson 2002).

We contribute to the methodological mission by developing a way of estimating public opinion in school districts that we call *small polity inference*. This technique begins with ten years of high-quality national opinion data concerning government spending on public education, broken down by states and demographics within states. The demographic breakdown permits us to estimate the average opinion for voters of certain "citizen types"—where a citizen type might be young, college-educated, suburban, African Americans living in Illinois. We combine traditional methods of simulated electorates (Pool, Abelson, and Popkin 1965; Weber and Shaffer 1972; Weber et al. 1972; Erikson 1978; Werner 1998), survey aggregation (Erikson, Wright, and McIver 1993; Brace et al. 2002), and Bayesian hierarchical models (Gelman and Little 1997; Park, Gelman, and Bafumi 2004) to estimate the spending preferences of various citizen types. Our method is explained in chapter 3, with a technical methodological discussion in appendix A. We then use U.S. Census data collected at the school district level to see the relative mix of the various citizen types in each American school district, producing a valid estimate of public opinion in each district. This allows us to do something that has never been done before: to compare preferences for spending with actual spending in nearly all American school districts.

Studying policy responsiveness also requires understanding how these preferences and wants are translated into policy outcomes. This requires working at the intersections of political theories concerning elections, citizen behavior, and governing structures. One of our most important missions as political scientists is to study how political institutions—rules of the game and political organizations—affect democratic governance. Some institutions enhance policy responsiveness while other governmental arrangements thwart the public's will and give undue influence to elites or organized interests. Our research can serve to inform those who would transform our governing institutions so that they become more democratic. For example, policies to reform and revise the way public education is funded and administered are constantly being considered in the American state capitals. Pennsylvania, for example, enacted in 2003 large-scale changes affecting the use of the property tax and school budget referenda, each of which we examine in detail in this book.

Finally, responsiveness studies address critical issues of normative political theory. In essence, every policy responsiveness study is a report card on how democratic the United States really is, and the results can lead to spirited debates (see the volume by Manza, Cook, and Page 2002). Though we often take it as a given that high levels of policy responsiveness are valued, the Progressive reformers of the early twentieth century who were so central to establishing the contemporary system of American public education were quite skeptical about ordinary citizens' ability to act in the public interest.

To others, however, public school governance typically embodies the "belief that local government is the most democratically legitimate government" (McDermott 1999, 13). Antifederalists believed this, de Tocqueville took note of it, and communitarians today continue to talk about it. This ideal runs particularly strong in thinking about public schools: More than any other level of government, school "governance is rooted in our beliefs in democratic control" (Wong 1995, 24), and the American school board has been idealized as "the crucible of democracy" (Iannaccone and Lutz 1995, 39).

These contradictory ideas about democratic control of public schools make the local school district a particularly appropriate level at which to examine policy responsiveness. In this book, we put these idealistic characterizations to the test. Do some types of school district governance, such as ward-based elections or referendum requirements, enhance responsiveness? Do other forms of governance limit the influence of less powerful groups, such as African Americans in the South? Are teachers' unions so powerful that they thwart the desires of local residents? How does the variety of ways we finance public education affect policy responsiveness and the power of organized interests? Are the elderly really a "Gray Peril" to public education funding? By examining school finance through the lens of policy responsiveness, we seek to ascertain how democratic these ten thousand democracies really are.

Acknowledgments

This book would not have been possible without the taxpayers of the United States. We rely heavily on information collected by the U.S. Census and by the U.S. Department of Education that is made freely available to all citizens. In addition, we received substantial support from the National Science Foundation (NSF). Additional financial support was provided by the Research and Graduate Studies Office of the College of the Liberal Arts at the Pennsylvania State University, with which we are both affiliated.

The extensive financial support from the NSF and from our university made it possible to hire a large number of outstanding consultants and research assistants. We appreciate the efforts of Stephen Matthews, director, and Steven Graham, senior consultant, at the Geographic Information Core of our Population Research Institute. Along with Donald Miller, a senior programmer at the institute, they provided invaluable assistance in dealing with large government data sets and ensuring proper matching of geographic areas.

We also worked with a large number of talented research assistants, including Amber Boydstun, Michael Fazio, Beth Klemick, Marcie Seiler, Daniel Jones White, and Nancy Wiefek. Steve Poyta of the U.S. Bureau of the Census was extremely helpful in locating and transmitting 1987 data on elected school board officials. We also received invaluable assistance from state school board associations around the country, who helped us navigate the complexity of district budget approval processes.

We received helpful comments from colleagues in our department, especially Frank Baumgartner, James Eisenstein, Quan Li, and Susan Welch. Our colleagues in Penn State's College of Education—Bill Boyd, David Baker, and Lisa Lattuca—were especially helpful in providing a disciplinary perspective.

We also were challenged and prodded by many colleagues who read early versions of the chapters in this book. We benefited from comments and suggestions made by participants at the annual meetings of the American Political Science Association, the Midwest Political Science Association, and especially the State Politics and Policy Conference—one of the best specialized gatherings in the profession. We thank Charles Barrilleaux, William Berry, Shaun Bowler, Paul Brace, Todd Donovan, Dick Engstrom, Elizabeth Gerber, Jeff Henig, David Lowery, Ron Weber, Gerry Wright, Dick Winters, and others we may have inadvertently neglected to mention.

We knew from our first meeting with Gail Grella of Georgetown University Press and Barry Rabe, then editor of its American Governance and Public Policy series, that we would write a better book if we worked with the press, and we were not disappointed. Throughout the editorial process, we were impressed with the skill and competence of the Georgetown editorial staff and the new series editors, Gerard Boychuk, Karen Mossberger, and Mark Rom. Finally, we thank Willa Silverman and Lee Ann Banaszak for their patience and support. This project began over dinner with the four of us, plus the kids, talking about the upcoming school board election. We dedicate it to our children, Ben, Clara, and Isaac, and to the fine public schools of the State College Area school district.

chapter one
Policy Responsiveness in American School Districts

There are over 14,000 school districts in the United States. They range from the Mohawk Valley school district in Arizona, where 254 students in kindergarten through the eighth grade are taught in one school, to the Los Angeles public school system, where close to 600,000 students in all grades are taught in more than 600 schools. Each of these districts, and the thousands in between, are governed and administered by a state-empowered school board. These boards make decisions about everything from after-school programs to teacher salaries, class sizes, and the teaching of creationism in the sixth grade. Among these are roughly 10,000 districts that educate students from kindergarten all the way through high school.

As much as school districts differ in their size, affluence, or curricula, they differ as well in the ways they are governed; indeed, in America's school districts and their governing boards we see the full scope and breadth of American local governance. It could not be any other way. Education has long been understood as a state responsibility but one equated with the American ideals of localism; the modern public schools have roots in colonial America, the western frontier, southern segregation, and the chaos of the early industrial city. The civil rights struggles of the 1960s have left their mark, as has the more recent emphasis on privatism and consumer choice.

We find, therefore, that some schools use town meetings inherited from Colonial America while some big-city governments achieve ethnic balance by appointing all school board members. School budgets in some areas are controlled by larger municipalities in ways that would seem familiar to a machine-era party boss, while in others school finances are completely separate from other government functions with dedicated revenue streams and public referenda on school budgets. In some communities, at-large voting continues to dilute minorities' electoral strength, while in others it may actually enhance it; across the range of electoral schemes, we find school boards that are representative of their populations and others so unrepresentative as to seem almost anachronistic.

Ten Thousand Democracies?

This wide range of governing strategies is the result of various American movements to reform governments in order to make them more effective. Each of these movements reflects their unique expression of the "democratic wish"—a phrase coined by James Morone to embody the idealism and celebration of "direct citizen participation in politics" (1998, 5). However, idealism frequently falls short of the mark, and governing reforms intended to empower ordinary citizens, such as referenda or town meetings, can sometimes have unintended consequences. Similarly, those intended to lessen the influence of corrupt city politicians can also lessen the influence of the ethnic and racial minorities those politicians may have represented. Thus it is an open question whether specific political arrangements are more or less democratic than others. In this book, we assess one important aspect of democracy in the nearly 10,000 districts that educate students from kindergarten through high school: the degree to which the financial policies adopted by school boards comport with the preferences of the citizens in those school districts. This correspondence is what political scientists and political sociologists refer to as *policy responsiveness.*

The *Democratic Wish* and Contemporary School Boards

James Morone's *The Democratic Wish* (1998) offers a broad historical treatment of how democratic idealism plays a recurring role in the creation of American political institutions. Therefore, while the New England colonists and their celebration of yeomen democracy are long gone, the town meeting remains in much of New England and more than 300 New England school districts continue to set their annual operating budgets and tax rates at town meetings.

The growth of America's cities and waves of immigration during the nineteenth century transformed urban governance and gave rise to urban political machines that governed through graft and elaborate patronage systems—but also provided services and political power to Roman Catholics and other minority groups that were otherwise excluded from Protestant centers of national political power. Schools were an important source of patronage jobs and of major public construction projects. Thus it is not surprising that many big cities retained public schools as an important responsibility of elected mayors and council members and that today roughly 200 American cities retain exclusive control over the funding and governance of their schools.

Outside New England and many large cities, the Progressive Movement of the late nineteenth and early twentieth centuries transformed all manner of local governments but none so much as those governing American public schools.[1] The Progressives' ideal of efficient and expert-led governance and education—the so-called one best system—was imposed incompletely on a patchwork of existing institutional forms, including one-room school districts, big-city schools, New England towns, and the growing suburbs (Tyack 1974).[2]

The Progressive Era politicians and school reformers believed that school governance would be more efficient if it were buffered from local control and the influence of political parties and powerful machine politicians (Tyack and Cuban 1995). They therefore advocated electoral reforms that would promote professionalism, expertise, and bureaucratic models of governance while insulating these professionals from the influence of ordinary citizens (Tyack 1974). This insulation was achieved primarily by detaching school governance from existing municipal governments, consolidating the smallest school districts into larger ones, and by promoting at-large elections that made it difficult for working-class citizens to compete effectively for political office. Yet Progressives also introduced public referenda that allowed those same ordinary citizens to directly participate in the decisions to increase spending and taxes. Today, the large majority of American school boards retain one, two, or more reforms promoted by the Progressives.

Institutional reforms were not, however, solely the legacy of the Progressives. Later in the twentieth century, civil rights advocates would insist upon greater minority representation, to give voice to and better represent the interests and preferences of minority residents. This was achieved by reversing the Progressive system of at-large elections in more than 2,000 school districts, enabling large gains in the election of African Americans to school boards during the 1980s and 1990s.

Citizen Participation in Public School Governance

Of course, New England colonists and Progressives have left the scene, big-city political machines have little resemblance to their nineteenth-century forebearers, and voting rights advocates may no longer fight the sorts of blatant racial discrimination of the 1950s and 1960s. Yet these groups have left their mark as contemporary school districts and governing boards retain the elements of different eras of institution building and present the widest imaginable range of ways to govern. In social-scientific terms, they represent an enormous natural laboratory within which to explore democracy and popular control of government policies. In this book, we will use this natural laboratory to examine policy responsiveness across the range of ways in which schools are governed. We will show that seemingly arcane choices about the ways that revenue is raised, school board members are selected, and financial linkages are maintained between school boards and their state and local governments have important implications for the voice that ordinary citizens have in the policymaking process.

Morone asks how institutions influenced by the democratic wish, as articulated and interpreted at different points in our history, facilitate or retard citizen participation in school district decisions. Our question is similar: How do these institutions facilitate or retard the translation of citizen desires into actual policies? As Page (1994, 25) and Manza and Cook (2002) have observed, assessing the *conditional* nature of policy responsiveness is the central unanswered question in the field.

This question has been a salient one for many students of municipal government. Indeed, they have studied some of the same sorts of Progressive-inspired governance structures—corporate models of governance, at-large and nonpartisan elections—that shaped public school governance. Public preferences, they contend, should be muted or amplified, and conflict deflected or engaged through the many different types of urban and local governing arrangements (Welch and Bledsoe 1988; Lineberry and Fowler 1967; Helig and Mundt 1984). Likewise, scholars working in the public choice tradition, which tries to identify the ideal conditions for matching majority preferences with government outcomes, frequently use local governments here and abroad to test their median voter models. These models posit that legislative and administrative bodies move policy outcomes away from public preferences toward those of elected officials, while institutions of direct democracy, such as the initiative and referenda, bypass these to achieve results more in line with voter preferences (e.g., Matsusaka 1995; Pommerehne 1978; Steunenberg 1992). These studies have moved the field forward but many, especially those based on local governments, share a major shortcoming: They do not attempt to measure public preferences directly but infer them based on proxy variables or simply make assumptions about public opinion. In this book, we assess the conditional nature of policy responsiveness directly, thereby contributing to our understanding about democratic institutions generally as well as showing how institutions play large, and sometimes surprising, roles in the politics of school finance.

What Determines Educational Spending Levels?

The amount spent on each pupil enrolled in a school district depends in large part on the local economic base, with affluent districts able to spend more than poorer districts. Other district characteristics play a role as well, including economies of scale from having large populations and the value of homes in the community. But economics is not everything, and in empirical studies local income and housing values never explain more than half the variation in school spending levels. For any given tax base, local school districts make choices in determining how much of that tax base to use for public education. The choices are *political* choices, and to explain them we need to understand political preferences, political institutions, and politically engaged interest groups.

Differences in economics and resources are therefore important, but they are not the primary focus of this book. There are some excellent treatments of state and school district financing and economic resources. We relied a good deal on the third edition of Allan Odden and Lawrence O. Picus's *School Finance: A Policy Perspective* (2004), Kenneth Wong's *Funding Public Schools: Politics and Policies* (1999), and Caroline Hoxby's articles (1996, 1998). Our goal, however, is to consider whether public opinion, political institutions, and interests lead to different funding levels among school districts with *comparable* levels of economics and resources. This may seem like a daunting task because it is difficult to ever find two or more school districts that are exactly alike. But the statistical analysis that we employ throughout the book allows us to do exactly this. All our multiple regression models *control* for the effects of economics and resources, allowing us to make exactly the sorts of comparisons we are most interested in making.

These same statistical techniques allow us to see whether other factors, in addition to local resources and public opinion, also affect spending decisions. For example, we also expect that various interest groups will try to influence tax rates and spending levels. Scholars and local school administrators agree that the two most important interests are teacher unions and senior citizens, and we will examine the extent to which these groups influence school budgets, how they do so, and whether their influence comes at the expense of ordinary citizens.

Finally, political institutions can have a large influence on school spending levels. We have discussed the wide variety of governing institutions that are present in the nation's school districts. Political scientists and economists have argued that some of these arrangements are, in effect, biased toward higher or lower spending. For example, many public choice scholars believe that institutions of direct democracy (initiatives and referenda) lead to lower overall spending levels, whereas others argue that certain tax regimes (i.e., reliance on property taxes) actually lead to higher spending.

Taking these different impacts of funding into account leads to both a simple and a conditional model of school finance and policy responsiveness. In figure 1.1, we depict a highly stylized version of the relationships we will be exploring. In most of our analyses, we will be trying to explain why spending is higher or lower in some districts than others. In the figure, the solid arrows represent our simple models of the factors that we believe cause differences in spending levels. This means that we expect economic resources, local citizen preferences, institutions, and interest groups to all play a direct and unmediated role in determining overall public school budgets.

The solid arrows in figure 1.1 correspond to what we call our *main effects* or direct causes of spending; the dashed arrows reflect our belief that institutions matter not only in contributing to higher or lower spending but also in giving ordinary citizens or interest groups greater or lesser voice in the policymaking process. These effects are *conditional* because the extent to which public opinion causes a change in public spending depends on, or is "conditioned by," the political institutions in the community—for example, whether they use budget referenda or town meetings. The role of public opinion will be greater in some school districts than in others because the governing mechanisms allow the public to be better represented when actual budget decisions are made.

Because we will be using statistical models to test these explanations, it is useful to consider these relationships in statistical modeling terms. A school district's spending level is the *dependent variable* that we want to explain. Levels of spending depend upon levels of our causal or *independent variables*. These are the factors, such as opinion, that we believe lead different school districts to spend different amounts. But these

Figure 1.1. Simple and Conditional Models of School Finance

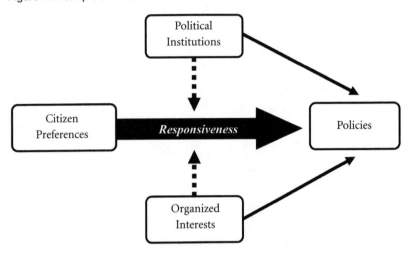

causes are conditioned by political institutions and, when one factor is conditioned by another, they are said to statistically *interact*. Fortunately, as we will see just below, these interactions can be expressed graphically, allowing us to see how the factors in figure 1.1 together shape local spending levels.

Overview of the Argument

The arrows and boxes in figure 1.1 each represent a complex political process, shaped by specific historical reforms, particular governing arrangements, and the various collection of interests "on the ground" in any particular school district. Each chapter in the book will focus on two or three aspects of the model.

Spending Levels

As we demonstrate in chapter 2, there are big differences in local spending on education across school districts within individual states and all districts in the country. Throughout our analysis, we use spending policies from 1995, the most recent year available for the special census data and spending data that we rely upon; but the basic relationships between groups, preferences, and institutions and spending policies should not have changed significantly since then. In 1995 the Blanchard school district in McClain County, Oklahoma, enrolled 882 students in twelve grades and spent $3,755 per student; that same year, the Valhalla Union school district in Westchester County, New York, a district nearly the same size, spent $13,454 for each student enrolled. That means that each classroom in Valhalla (if we assume a classroom has twenty-five students), has an additional quarter million dollars in resources—although we certainly would not expect classrooms in Valhalla to be as large as those in Blanchard.

Local spending patterns within states are not as dramatic as those across states, because of state court and political pressures to equalize spending, but differences can still be great. As we show in chapter 2, local educational spending is highly responsive to community-level economic resources such as income level and housing values. But many other factors, including the relative roles of the local school board and the state government, matter as well. Further, in some states local school districts are responsible for more of their own spending decisions than in others. These *funding regime* decisions are of critical importance to spending levels, the political dynamics, and the influence of public opinion and interest groups. We will begin, therefore, by portraying the landscape of educational financing in the United States and introduce some of the data used by us and educational finance specialists to compare educational spending.

Public Opinion

Even the best statistical analysis of school financing can explain only some of the differences in per-pupil spending across states when they incorporate only the fiscal resources of the district and state. These require as well a consideration of public preferences or, as economists often call it, "taste" for educational spending. We demonstrate in chapter 3 that dozens of public opinion polls conducted in various states and nationally show consistently that most people want to spend more on the public schools and support for increased spending has risen dramatically during the past three decades. Further, we demonstrate that there are important differences in the demographic profile of higher and lower spenders that are also consistent across many state and national polls. This information is both critical to understanding education politics and essential to our ability to estimate public opinion at the district level.

Measuring Public Opinion

Assessing the opinion–policy linkage and the mediating role of institutions requires measures of attitudes toward spending on public schools at the school district level. We need to rank each of the roughly 10,000 unified, kindergarten through twelfth grade (K–12), school districts from extremely conservative (the majority feels that school spending and school taxes are already too high) to extremely liberal (the majority wants to spend more on schools even if this requires a tax increase). Ranking constituencies in this way has been the major challenge facing all responsiveness studies, and the challenge is formidable when the constituencies are small and numerous. It would be impossible to field an identical survey in each school district. With as few as 300 interviews per district, we would require roughly 3 million interviews (on the cheap, at perhaps $30 per completed interview, such an undertaking would cost close to $100 million).

Our method of estimating public opinion in each school district is called *small polity inference* and we introduce this in chapter 3. In brief, we generate spending preference scores in each school district based upon a detailed demographic profile of the community and a detailed individual-level model of spending preferences. In other words, first we identify the spending preferences of various *citizen types*; for example, a suburban, black college graduate in Georgia or a white, urban high school graduate in California. We then see the proportion of each citizen type residing in each school district. In chapter 3, we provide considerable evidence that our measure is a valid indicator of public preferences toward spending on schools and that it correlates very highly with parallel measures that use the well-accepted methods developed by Erikson, Wright, and McIver (1993) in their work on state-level public opinion.

Policy Responsiveness

Armed with a valid measure of local opinion, we can assess how closely spending levels track with public preferences. We show that within states, liberal districts spend considerably more than conservative districts with identical financial resources. Yet our more probing analyses seek to identify the types of governmental arrangements that promote especially high or especially low levels of correspondence. In addition, we seek to understand how two key interests—teacher unions and elderly voters—are also able to influence policies in ways that may thwart or reinforce the preferences of the majority of citizens.

This analytic approach builds on the major studies of policy responsiveness (e.g., Miller and Stokes 1963; Erikson, Wright, and McIver 1993; Page and Shapiro 1992). Public opinion is treated as a cause (an independent variable) of local spending levels (our primary dependent variable). If districts containing more pro-spending citizens actually spend more than economically similar districts with more low-tax citizens, we will conclude that governments are responsive to their citizens' preferences. The stronger the relationship—in statistical terms, the steeper the slope or the larger the regression coefficient between opinion and policy outcomes—the more responsive the governments are.

Governing Institutions

Even without any consideration of institutions and interest groups, we show in chapter 3 that public opinion has a strong correspondence with actual policies within most states. But the heart of the book moves well beyond this simple generalization as we start thinking theoretically and empirically about when and where opinion should most matter. Only then do we begin to see the full picture of policy responsiveness in American school districts.

We demonstrate in chapter 4, for example, that in New England many school districts still use the colonial town meeting. Though the town meeting is often praised for intimately involving the public in decision making, we actually find that, for a variety of reasons, it does nothing to help translate public opinion into policy. It may be a great democratic experience for those who participate, but this participation requires a high cost borne by only a few, and the result may be policy that is, ironically, not particularly responsive to the public's desire for more or less spending.

Yet it is the Progressives who are of most interest to us in chapter 4 because of their overwhelming influence on American local government and school boards. Some of the Progressive efforts can seem like "reform oxymorons" (Morone 1998, 6). For example, the effort to "restore power to the people" through referenda would suggest that responsiveness is enhanced in the many districts that allow direct voting on districts or budgets; but this contrasts with the "distinctly undemocratic administrative reforms" (p. 26), such as the use of expert, independent boards separated from public input. In each case, we explore the extent to which different means of allowing the public access to the decision-making process does or does not interfere with the translation of public preferences into policy outcomes.

We continue this approach by considering electoral mechanisms in chapter 5. Most American polities, including school districts, rely far more upon indirect, representative democracy than they do direct democracy like the referendum. The vast majority of the roughly 95,000 school board directors and members are chosen through elections, although a fair number are appointed as well, and the rules that govern these elections are, we contend, critical to policy responsiveness. They are especially critical when we consider the way electoral systems have been used throughout American history to suppress minority voting and representation.

Working within that tradition, we explore how these rules and electoral schemes used by school boards affect their racial composition. But we go one step further and consider how they affect policy responsiveness. As with other local governments, the electoral systems of American school districts, particularly but not exclusively in the southern

United States, have come under scrutiny from legislators and courts. Provisions of the Voting Rights Act meant to prevent the dilution of minority votes have been applied to school board elections as well. In chapter 5, we consider the three major methods of choosing school board members: appointments, at-large, and district elections. We also place these methods in the context of each district's racial composition. And by comparing elections of minority representatives before and after some school districts switched from at-large to district elections, we show how electoral systems shape both who is elected and how responsive they are.

Interest Groups

Teachers' unions are the most organized of the major interest groups seeking to influence educational policies in the United States. The Hoover Institution's Terry Moe believes that their enormous memberships and financial resources give them power that is unrivaled by any other active player in local or state education politics (Moe 2003). Moe sees teachers' unions as impediments to reform and costly to taxpayers because they inflate local and state education costs for their own career and financial interests. But they are not the only interest with a systematic impact on local education spending.

Scholars, policymakers, and educators often seem certain that high concentrations of older citizens constitute a "Gray Peril" (Rosenbaum and Button 1989) to school funding. Chuck Fest, the onetime president of the Mount Laurel (New Jersey) Education Association, perhaps captured best the fears of many when he characterized elderly voters as "old coots" who should be given a roll of quarters and shipped off to Atlantic City on election day (Coles 1997). Although often unorganized and fairly small in number, the elderly also are understood by many to be an important interest in local school politics whose preoccupation with property taxes and lack of direct interest in neighborhood schools lead them to oppose additional spending.

There is nothing inherently undemocratic about school spending policies reflecting the preferences of teachers, seniors, or any other group. To *pluralist* theorists, policy is and probably should be made through the ongoing struggle of groups and interests. Even Madison, writing as Publius in the *Federalist Papers*, discusses competing factions as an inevitable fact of political life. But if the elderly or unions exert an influence out of proportion to their numbers in their community, school boards may fail to be responsive to their broader public. Critics of pluralism often raise concerns that groups' control over resources and their access to elected officials make them too powerful relative to the public interest.

Understanding the role of these two prominent interests is a central task for us in this book. By utilizing specialized data collections from the U.S. Census, we are able to take a new look at these interests across the entire scope of the nation, going beyond the majority of studies that are confined to a single state or community. In each case, we probe the conditions under which we should really expect each to have the pernicious effects that their opponents seem to anticipate. We reconsider and revise the Gray Peril thesis by distinguishing between those who are new to a community and have few ties to the local schools and those who may have loyalty to a school district that has been a part of their lives for a long time. For teachers' unions, it means distinguishing between unions at the state and local levels and looking at when and how they should be powerful.

We also demonstrate that the political influence of each of these interests can only be understood within the context of the state *funding regime*. States approach the financing of public education differently. In some, spending on education is more of a state than a local responsibility; in others, localities are expected to take on a larger share. Within these regimes, states employ different formulas to determine which localities will receive more or less state funds, while localities and states together determine the type of tax that can be used to finance neighborhood schools and may give tax rebates to specific groups. These, too, are important institutional rules of the games. And they determine where interests can and will be influential. Unions, we show, have a keen sense of whether their activism should be directed at the state or local level, and this decision has implications for their influence. And the elderly, we show, are much less influential where the property tax is either not used or remedied through tax credits and circuit breakers.

Conclusion

States spend more on education than they do on anything else and have created more than 14,000 special local governments, called school districts, with the sole responsibility of administering K–12 education for them. A small number of school districts are governed by the community's municipal government (typically a city council or town meeting), but most districts are governed by school boards that must determine how much to spend on community schools and how much local revenue they will need. The amount each district spends is determined to a large degree by the resources available to it by taxable income and property. This leads many communities, especially better-off ones, to fight hard to preserve a large local role for what is essentially a state function. This localism is a distinguishing feature of American public education.

These school boards have been touched by the important political ideas and movements of modern American political history. Although most reflect the priorities and administrative ideals of the Progressives, a substantial number retain the town meeting format of Colonial America, and others have been relatively untouched since their original creation as extensions of other municipal governments. Their modes of selecting school board members or directors vary widely, and many school districts revised their electoral systems in response to the voter rights movements codified in the Voting Rights Act of 1965. School boards and districts have felt the impact of these and other historical periods, making them a diverse and theoretically rich set of political institutions.

This book is, in a sense, a tour across space and across two centuries of historical legacies. The tour is a specialized one—examining the performance of American democracy through the lens of the choices

Americans have made about funding their public schools. We begin in chapter 2, where we explore in detail the local and state financing of public education.

Notes

1. Richard Hofstadter describes Progressivism as the "broader impulse toward criticism and change that was everywhere so conspicuous after 1900. . . . Its general theme was the effort to restore a type of economic individualism and political democracy that was widely believed to have existed in earlier America and to have been destroyed by the great corporation and corrupt political machine" (1965, 5).

2. On the characterization of the early American state as a patchwork of courts and parties, see Skowronek (1982).

chapter two
Financing Public Education

In the early 1800s, the citizens in many American towns established local systems of public education. Yet by the beginning of the twentieth century, K–12 education had become a responsibility of the states (Strang 1987, 354). The federal government's role, conversely, has always been small. Even though education is discussed by presidential candidates and Congress periodically passes major legislation, no more than 10 percent of public school revenues has ever come from the federal government.[1] Moreover, the U.S. Supreme Court has held that education is not a fundamental right guaranteed in the federal Constitution.[2]

The action in public education, especially in the financing and administration of American schools, is in the states and the more than 14,000 school districts they have created. Unlike the federal Constitution, nearly all the state constitutions explicitly provide for a free education. The language in the Idaho constitution is typical: "It shall be the duty of the legislature of Idaho to establish and maintain a general, uniform and thorough system of public, free common schools" (article 9, section 1).[3] By the early 1990s, education financing systems of most of the states had been challenged in state courts, with about half found in conflict with the state constitutions (Odden and Picus 2004). In nearly all these cases, the courts addressed the question of whether constitutional guarantees were satisfied when education spending varied widely across the state's school districts.

As we will show, state governments responded by changing how they finance public education. State systems that were nearly totally reliant upon the revenues raised by local school districts took on a larger share of funding responsibility. This has gone a long way toward reducing intrastate differences in spending, but it has not eliminated them (Odden and Picus 2004; Hoxby 1998; Hertert, Busch, and Odden 1994), and local school districts retain substantial financial control.

Not surprisingly, districts with affluent families spend more than districts serving poorer citizens, which leads to large intrastate differences in school spending levels. However, wealth and property values explain at most half the variation in per-pupil spending (Feldstein 1975; Hoxby 1998). Local communities and school boards make critical decisions about their *tax effort*—how much to extract from available wealth (Odden and Picus 2004; Hoxby 1998)—and these decisions are also relevant to understanding persistent inequalities. The revenues extracted by any given community, though obviously not independent of fiscal capacity, are shaped as well by community preferences, the institutional rules of the community school board, and the state financing system in which they operate. We address these in subsequent chapters but begin here by exploring the educational financing system.

The Evolution of American School Districts

The Progressive reformers of the late nineteenth and early twentieth centuries viewed community control of schools as a serious impediment to improving public education. At the turn of the century, there were 200,000 one-room schoolhouses and tens of thousands of small, multi-school systems. The Progressives were skeptical that the ordinary citizens who hired their local teacher (or teachers), set policy, and raised revenues for these schools were up to the task. They therefore set in motion a seventy-year process of consolidation that combined smaller schools into larger ones (Tyack 1974). At the same time, state governments created smaller (five- or seven-member) school boards to govern these larger districts while installing more professional, independent superintendents. These reforms were intended to introduce a corporate model to school administration (Tyack 1974) with beneficial economies of scale and replacement of local politics with the "rationalities of formal organization" (Strang 1987, 352).

Consolidation advocates were interested in eliminating differences in how schools were governed, how teachers were trained, and what was taught and they were not particularly concerned with the equalizing the resources available to each school system. But though consolidation was never intended to reduce funding differences between school districts, it nonetheless had some impact on them. The reason is that small school districts are more likely to include people of similar economic circumstances than are larger districts. Because larger districts are more likely to include people of different economic circumstances, there should be smaller differences between them, thereby reducing revenue differences. Consolidation brought unlike districts together—much to the disappointment of many communities, which saw their local schools as a source of local pride and cohesion (Tyack 1974)—and must have reduced financial differences across the state.

Figure 2.1 traces this consolidation along with several other key trends in school governance and finance. The vertical bars record how the number of school districts declined from over 110,000 in 1939 to roughly the present level of more than 14,000 by 1970. The lines show changes in the percentage of revenues from local, state, and federal levels of government.

Equity and the Increasing Role for the States in Local Educational Finance

At about the time that consolidation had run its course, the California court decision in *Serano v. Priest* (1971) changed the landscape in California and, in subsequent years, in other states as well. In a wideranging decision, the California Supreme Court supported new legal arguments developed to address funding inequities. The court found California's financing system to be unconstitutional and held that education was a fundamental state right. Specifically, districts with significantly less property wealth were identified as a "suspect class" entitled to constitutional protections. But, though clearly connecting funding

Figure 2.1. Key Trends in the Evolution of American School Districts, 1939–99

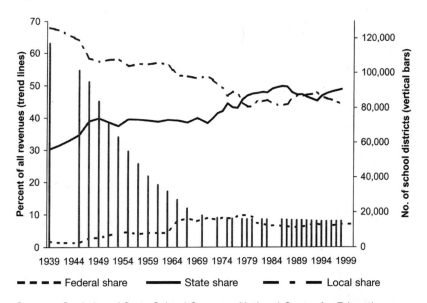

Sources: Statistics of State School Systems, National Center for Education Statistics, U.S. Department of Education; Revenues and Expenditures for Public Elementary and Secondary Education; and Common Core of Data Surveys.

inequities to local reliance on the property tax, the California court did not go so far as to say that the use of the local property tax to fund education was, in itself, unconstitutional (Odden and Picus 2004). The property tax remains today the main source of local school revenues.

Serano would be followed by other decisions in California as well as New Jersey, and by 1991 in more than forty other states. In more than twenty states, funding systems were completely or partially overturned. Responding to the demands of these rulings and ongoing threats of litigation, state legislatures sought ways to equalize spending across their school districts, in most cases without removing schools from local control or denying localities their use of the property tax. As they have often done in other policy areas (Peterson 1995), states took on this redistributive role by assuming a greater financing responsibility. Most states chose to do this by distributing funds directly to school districts along territorial lines rather than to particular categories of students classified through social categories such as income or need.[4] Most states adopted "foundation" programs that distributed tax dollars inversely to local taxing capacity or wealth while guaranteeing each district a foundation or minimum level of per-pupil spending.[5] States could therefore reduce inequalities without "undermining local autonomy in instructional and curricular matters" (Wong 1999, 83).

Figure 2.1 shows this second transformation of state education systems as well: After remaining unchanged from the 1940s to 1970, states became responsible for ever larger shares of local school spending in the fifteen years following the *Serano* decision. The federal government increased its role in the 1960s by pursuing social redistributive goals such as promoting racial integration, the educational rights of the handicapped, and inequities that "arise primarily from class, status and racial differences" (Wong 1999, 18). By the 1980s its total share was back where it had been earlier in the century. Consolidation continues today in some states, and others continue to respond to legal and political challenges to their funding distribution.[6] The overall state–local balance, however, has been fairly stable since the early 1980s. Yet this overall stability hides persistent cross-state differences in how states redistribute and participate in education financing.

State Funding Regimes

These differences are represented in figure 2.2, which shows the *local* financing responsibility across all of a state's unified school districts in 1995.[7] For each state there is a vertical white line, a box, and a thinner horizontal line capped with a cross-hatch. The white line represents the proportion of revenues raised from local sources for the median school district in each state. In Washington State, for example, the median school district relies upon local revenues for 20 percent of all local education revenues—half the districts in Washington rely on local spending for more than 20 percent of their revenues and half rely on local spending for less than 20 percent (most of the rest comes from the state, and a small portion comes from the federal government). This differs dramatically from Massachusetts and New Hampshire, where the median school district derives 80 percent and nearly 100 percent, respectively, from local resources. There is wide variation in the extent to which states expect localities to assume responsibility for funding their community schools.

This is only part of the picture of how states fund K–12 public education. The shaded boxes and remaining lines, known as the "box and whiskers," give us additional information, showing how the rest of the districts within each state are distributed around this median.[8] The box end lines represent what are called "Tukey hinges" (named for John Wilder Tukey, who created this and other innovative ways to describe data visually), and they are drawn roughly at the 25th and 75th percentiles, meaning that one-quarter of the districts fall above the right-hand line and one-quarter fall below the left-hand line. The length of the box, therefore, shows the spread, or variability, of the data; the longer the box, the larger the distribution of values.

The location of the median line within the box indicates whether the distribution is such that cases are spread out widely among values higher than the median but bunched together below the median (positively skewed with the median toward the left-hand side of the box) or negatively skewed so that values are spread out below the median but bunched above it (median closer to the right-hand side of the box). The lines on either end of the box, the whiskers, are anchored by the largest and smallest observed values that are not outliers, defined here as more than 1.5 box lengths from the 75th or 25th percentiles. This gives us additional information about the nature of the distribution. In Wisconsin, for example, most districts raised between 40 and 60 percent of school revenues themselves, a fairly tight distribution. But a small number of districts are responsible for as much as 90 percent or as little as 10 percent of total revenues in the district.

The states are sorted in figure 2.2 according to the median value and run from those that rely the least on local governments to provide their own revenues to those that rely the most on localities. They show the rich variety in state funding regimes. Hawaii is the only state in the

Figure 2.2. State Funding Regimes: Percent of School District Revenues Raised Locally, 1995

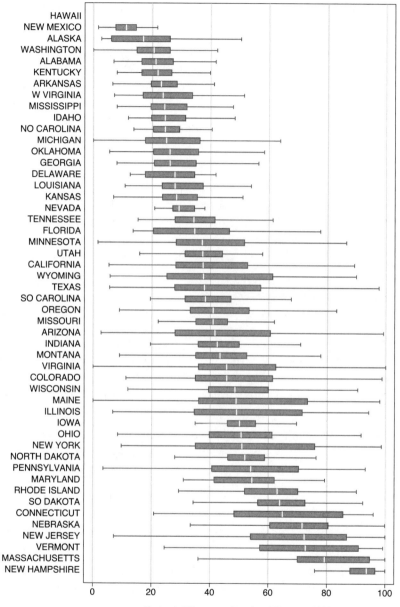

Percent of Revenues from Local Sources, 1995

Source: 1995 Local Education Agency Finance Survey, distributed by National Center for Educational Statistics.

union with nearly total state financing and operates with only one school district that encompasses the entire state. Other states offer less extreme examples of what Wong (1999) refers to as state dominance in school financing. In New Mexico, for example, the local school districts are responsible for a small share of funding for their local schools, with a median of only 11 percent of all revenues coming from local sources. West Virginia is similarly state dominant (median = 22.6), but with significant variation in the amount that it provides to its districts. In nearly all states, funds are distributed through a "leveling-up strategy" designed to "favor localities with low property values and high tax burdens" (Wong 1999, 72). Therefore, what we see in West Virginia is a greater effort at redistribution than in New Mexico. Though we cannot tell from figure 2.2 whether a district is a wealthy one or not, median income is strongly correlated with the percentage of local contributions to revenues ($r = 0.51$).

However, redistribution based on district need is most apparent in those states that allow localities to retain a large share of funding. In these states, there is a wide range in the percentage of aid provided by the state government to localities. And we presume, although we cannot tell from sure from this figure, that those receiving the largest percentage of state aid are the poorest. Conversely, those able to maintain the largest local share should be the wealthiest. In New Jersey, for example, the median is close to 80 percent local financing but the distribution is negatively skewed; the box and whiskers extend all the way to the point at which districts use as little 10 percent or less of their own funds, which shows that poorer districts receive a substantial percentage of their funds from the state.

A closer inspection of districts in New Jersey, New York, and New Hampshire is provided in figure 2.3. Here, district affluence is captured by the horizontal axis (wealthier districts to the right), and local responsibility for revenue is plotted on the vertical axis. The figures show that after a certain point wealthier districts in New York and New Jersey are unlikely to receive any additional state funds—they have, in effect, reached their foundation level. They are on their own to extract what-

Figure 2.3. Funding Regimes in Three States: The Relationship between District Per Capita Income and School Revenues Raised Locally, 1995

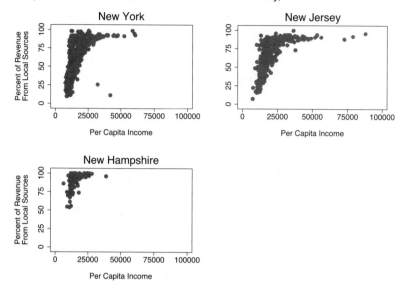

Source: Common Core of Data, National Center for Educational Statistics.

ever level of tax effort they desire or are able to fund their schools. At the low end, however, the relationship between local share and local income is very strongly correlated. In New Hampshire, conversely, localities both retain significant local control over revenues and are unlikely, in any case, to receive significant state aid to equalize funding disparities.

The Property Tax and Policy Responsiveness

A state's educational funding regime is important because the venue in which political issues are decided matters a great deal. At the state level, education spending is considered in context with other state priorities. As a result, education-related interest groups must compete with other well-organized interests from the business, labor, and nonprofit sectors. As we will demonstrate in chapter 6, in more state-centralized funding regimes, state teachers' unions are more influential than local ones. And though the purpose of state foundation programs is to assure all districts a minimal level of funding and to promote more equal spending across districts, one of their consequences could be a *lower* overall level of state funding than if decisions were relatively more localized.[9] In contrast, at the local level, education competes with other functions only in the small number of *dependent* districts (1,165) where financing responsibility typically rests with a town, city, or county government rather than solely with the school district. In the majority of American communities, school districts are *fiscally independent* and assume local funding responsibility themselves.

Perhaps the most critical consequence of relying more upon state than local spending is that it disconnects education funding from the local property tax. Nearly all communities rely upon these taxes to fund their public schools. In the view of many economists, the property tax is a true benefit tax that encourages local citizens to make "good" fiscal decisions (Oates 2001, 21; see also Fischel 2001b). In other words, the tax reflects the true cost of the benefits provided to the local residents who bear the tax. Because of this, the cost of the tax is nearly fully capitalized into the value of a home, which is to say that "the benefits from such things as superior schools and low crime rates, on the one hand, and low tax rates, on the other, tend to manifest themselves in the price of local dwellings" (Oates 2001, 22).[10] People will pay more for a home in a district with higher property taxes because the tax directly benefits their schools. This is one reason, according to Fischel (2001b), that school expenditures decline as states take on increasing burdens for financing. Residents are less interested in spending on education if it goes to communities other than their own, which is of course why redistribution is a state and not a local responsibility.

We expect that reliance upon the property tax will enhance the responsiveness of local government leaders to constituent preferences. A little economic theory is useful to understanding why. Charles Tiebout's "Pure Theory of Local Expenditures" (1956) basically says that people, when they can, will move to the community that provides them with the level of spending and benefits that they prefer. Because local governments can also control the makeup of their community through zoning, individuals cannot settle in a community where they receive more in benefits than they are willing to pay in taxes (Fischel 2001b).

Policy outcomes, therefore, will be very close to preferences of the residents but not necessarily because governments are actively responding to these preferences. Rather, people might settle in the communities that match their preferences but then have little political impact once they get there. Fischel, however, contends that the property tax introduces political responsiveness into this Tiebout world of people voting only with their feet because "Homeowners want local land use regulations to maximize the value of their homes." The property tax helps to make residents interested in the value of other people's property as well as their own and keeps residents connected and interested in their local government and in government spending. Indeed, Fischel argues that "the median voter rules in local governments" more than at other levels of government because of the property tax (2001b, 49).

Therefore, the extent to which a community is responsible for its own funding through the property tax should have an impact upon both spending levels and policy responsiveness. This will vary across states, because they establish different funding regimes, and across districts within a state because, as we have seen, wealthier districts are responsible for more of their own revenues. In a community with little local funding through the property tax, people may be disconnected from their schools and less supportive of them. In fact, Fischel goes so far as to argue that the *Serano* decision in California brought about the state's "Proposition 13" revolt against property taxes. More generally, decisions like *Serano* that led to the assumption of greater state responsibility weakened support for property taxes because school finance "had been effectively divorced from local tax bases" (Fischel 2002, 102).

The essence of all these arguments is that the funding regime is an important contextual and direct factor in explaining the amount of money school districts spend on the schools. They shape the venue in which political battles are fought. They determine how different interests are affected by educational spending decisions; for example, because the property tax most affects those on fixed incomes, groups such as the elderly should be a more potent political force where property taxes are more critical to local spending. They shape the context in which public preferences should or should not play a large role. And they even have an impact on how we look at the importance of resources to pay for education. When districts rely less on the property tax, housing values are less important in determining the amount of resources available to the local school district. We will return to these issues in later chapters as we explore responsiveness, interest group pluralism, and spending levels.

Per-Pupil Spending

Of course, the state courts were not interested in issues of governmental responsiveness to citizen's desires but rather in disparities in the amounts of money spent on students in districts within each state. The earliest cases relied on the equal protection clauses of state and federal constitutions to assess the constitutionality of the very unequal distribution of resources from one school district to the next. Later cases appealed to state education clauses and concluded that students in some districts were not receiving an "adequate" and guaranteed level of educational services (Odden and Picus 2004, 46). Jonathon Kozol brought these inequities to life in *Savage Inequalities* (1991). He compared relatively affluent suburban schools with schools like the one in East Saint Louis where a physics teacher showed Kozol his students' lab and lamented that "it would be great if we had water" (p. 27).

There is a lively debate in the educational finance literature about how these financial disparities affect education outcomes and whether greater resources improve educational quality. Gary Burtless (1996) introduces an authoritative book of essays on whether "money matters" and concludes that, in most cases, it probably does not. Hanushek's (1996) review of 377 published studies on the link between resources and student performance is a bit more muted but still hardly enthusiastic about the need to spend more in districts with fewer resources.

But though some economists and policy analysts remain unconvinced about the importance of resources to school performance, most educators, politicians, parents, and courts clearly prefer better-funded schools. We will see in chapter 3, for example, that most people would rather spend more and few want to spend less money on public schools. Homes sell for more where the schools are better (Weimer and Wolkoff 2001), and homeowners want to maintain quality schools because these directly affect the value of their homes (Fischel 2001a).

Further, several courts have explicitly linked resources with educational quality when they take an "adequacy" approach to state educational equity. The Kentucky Supreme Court, for example, found in 1989 that "students in property poor districts receive inadequate and inferior educational opportunities as compared to those offered to those students in the more affluent districts" (cited in Wong 1991, 134). The ruling in a New Jersey court decision was similar, and the reaction of parents and educators was even more revealing about the importance many place on resources: "The record demonstrates," wrote the court, "that poor urban school districts are unable to achieve comparability because of defects in the funding system." In summarizing the comments of parents and administrators in better-funded New Jersey districts (which were opposed to state equalization), Kozol clearly shows that they strongly believe that money "is crucial to rich districts but will be of little difference to the poor" (Kozol 1991, 169–71).

Instructional Expenditures

We will be looking at these spending differences throughout the book. Each year every local school board must develop and approve a school budget. To compare these across districts, we compute a measure of educational expenditures. The measure is expressed as dollars spent for each enrolled student. This measure of *per-pupil expenditures* does not include transportation costs (on average, about 4 percent of the typical district's budget) because they are a function of density or even desegregation orders requiring busing (Odden and Picus 2004) and therefore largely outside the discretion of either school boards or the public. Capital expenditures are also excluded, which make up about 8 percent of a typical budget.[11]

The largest category of educational spending per pupil is teacher salaries and benefits (about 60 percent of the total), with the remainder devoted to support staff, administration, upkeep of facilities, books, computers, and instructional materials and programs. During the past several decades, expenditures on teachers have increased steadily in real dollars, reflecting both higher salaries and smaller classes (Hanushek 1996). But the rate of overall instructional spending has been higher still, and most of the excess growth over that period has been spent on books, materials, and aides (Odden and Picus 2004, 301).

Figure 2.4 describes per-pupil educational expenditures for each state in 1995, using the same type of box-and-whisker graph seen earlier in the chapter. In figure 2.4, and throughout the book, we restrict ourselves to unified school districts; that is, those districts offering instruction in grades K–12. This allows for a meaningful comparison across districts. Again, the box-and-whisker format allows us to compare how districts within states compare with one another and how these overall distributions vary across states. Consistent with other studies (Evans, Murray, and Schwab 2001), we see that disparities between the states are slightly greater than within them; note the relative positions of the white lines, as well as the end lines, of each state's graph with the others, as well as the relatively small size of the boxes within each state. Of course, we expect this, because redistribution has come from the states rather than the federal government.

But even with state equalization efforts, the principle of horizontal equity—that "spending should be equal across school districts and schools" (Odden and Picus 2004, 63)—is clearly violated. In fourteen states, the distance between the top 25 percent and the bottom 25 percent of districts is more than $1,500 per student (or, in more concrete terms, a difference of $36,000 per classroom of twenty-four students).[12] Despite the efforts of state legislatures and the courts, spending variations remain.

Figure 2.4. Per-Pupil Instructional Expenditures by State, 1995 (dollars)

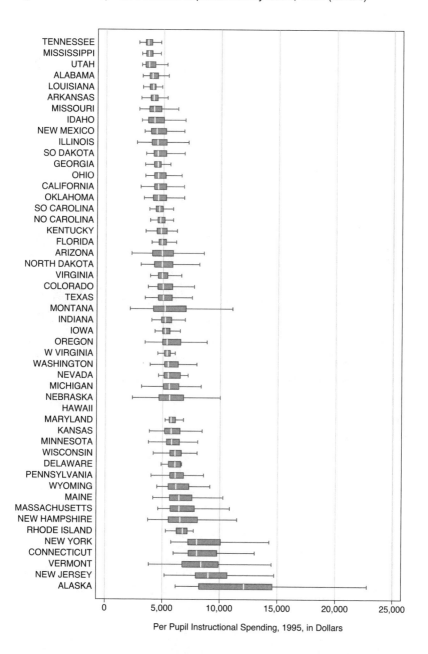

Per Pupil Instructional Spending, 1995, in Dollars

Source: 1995 Local Education Agency Finance Survey, distributed by National Center for Educational Statistics.

Conclusion

Funding regimes differ across the American states. When public schools were begun at the community level more than a century ago, they were funded almost entirely through local sources. Throughout the twentieth century, states took on more and more responsibility for providing K–12 education. Nearly all states expect localities to fund at least some significant amount of local education, but some state funding regimes retain far more localism than others. Within states, wealthier school districts are generally expected to pay more of their own way; but, again, funding regimes differ in how much states attempt to equalize spending by using state funds to make up for the revenue limitations of less well-off districts.

This distribution shapes the context within which politics operates. It determines the policymaking venue in which interests compete. And it determines the extent to which the property tax will be a critical political issue at the local level. Within districts, the property tax continues to be the dominant source of education funds. Even states with the most aggressive equalization plans allow wealthier districts to use their own funds so that the better-off districts spend more on their children's education. Despite the inequities in spending that result from reliance upon it, state and national courts have never found the property tax to be an unacceptable mechanism for raising education funds. Though differences within states in the amount districts spend are not as great as they once were, they are still significant.

Yet all this begs the question of how much local residents *want* to spend on their schools and the corresponding levels of taxation they are willing to endorse. Local property values and wealth alone can explain only a portion of the variation in per-pupil spending across districts (Murray, Evans, and Schwab 1998; Ladd 1975; Hoxby 1998). As Stanley Elam, the longtime director of Phi Beta Kappa's annual Survey of Public Attitudes toward the Public Schools, has argued "public opinion, in the last analysis, is what distinguishes the possible from the impossible in public education" (Elam 1995, 1). This has never before been explored at the local level. We will show that Elam is correct, and that public opinion plays an important role in creating spending differences across school districts that have comparable levels of economic resources. To demonstrate the important role of public opinion, however, we first need to answer several questions: Do most Americans support spending more on the public schools, or do they think current spending levels are adequate? Who are most in favor of spending increases, and who are most likely to oppose them? How can we use available polls to estimate public opinion in each of the nation's school districts? Chapter 3 answers each of these questions.

Notes

1. The most recent major legislation passed by Congress is the No Child Left Behind Act of 2001, which imposed a range of mandates tied to federal money on states and school districts to encourage early childhood education, provide student and school progress reports to parents, and prioritize the employment of qualified teachers.

2. This was in the case *Rodriguez v. San Antonio School District*, 411 U.S. 45 (1972). The Court held in a 5–4 decision that the Texas system of public schools did not violate the federal Constitution and that underfunded school districts are not a suspect class entitled to constitutional protection (Odden and Picus 2004).

3. A table of the forty-two states in which there have been court challenges to state education systems by 2004 can be found on the web page of Odden and Picus (2004; http://highered.mc-graw-hill.com/sites/0072823186/student_view0/table_of_school_finance_legal_.html). For each of the forty-two states, the relevant clause from the state constitution is reprinted.

4. In an analysis of eighteen states, Wong (1999) finds that 86 percent of state education expenditures in the period 1988–90 went to reducing interdistrict inequities and 7.8 percent went to addressing social inequities. The remainder was not used to equalize funding.

5. Foundation grants can be traced back to what was probably the first state redistributive effort in New York in the 1920s. But generally, prior to the 1970s, states relied much more on non-equity flat grants. These flat grants declined from 30 percent of total state aid in 1972 to only 14 percent in 1988. Flat grants guarantee an equal amount of state aid dollars per district.

6. There is still consolidation some among rural districts, but it proceeds at a much slower pace (Strang 1987). On recent consolidation, see "In Rural Utah, Students' School Day Stretches to 12 Hours (with 4 on the Bus)," *New York Times*, May 28, 2004.

7. The federal share is fairly small but disproportionate across states, so though the state share is highly and negatively correlated with the local share, it is not an exact mirror of it.

8. The median is a desirable measure of central tendency because it is not distorted by outliers or extreme values. Figure 2.2 uses unified (i.e., K–12) school districts only, and we have eliminated from this and subsequent analyses any school district with fewer than 250 students. Box-and-whisker plots often display outliers and extreme values, but the ones in this book do not.

9. Downes and Shah (1995) demonstrate that in many but not all cases the shift to state-level funding can lead to a general decrease in educational expenditures, a finding confirmed by

Fischel (2001b) and Silva and Sonstelie (1995). But Murray, Evans, and Schwab (1998) and Hoxby (1998) find otherwise.

10. There are competing views of whether the property tax is the true benefit tax that Fischel argues it is (Oates 2001; Zodrow 2001). But there is little dispute that education costs are at least partially capitalized into the value of a home (Zodrow 2001).

11. Capital spending is more relevant to school board politics than transportation spending. However, this budget category from the National Center for Educational Statistics data includes debt interest as well as the value of educational capital acquired or created during the year, regardless of whether the outlay was financed by borrowing or current revenues. Because the political process for selling bonds and borrowing money is different in most districts than is the process for passing the school operating budget, we choose to exclude these expenditures from the per-pupil expenditures we use to assess responsiveness. In nearly all states, bonds are voted upon by the public under at least some conditions, but as we will see in chapter 4, district residents vote on school budgets in only some states under different conditions.

12. The coefficient of variation, the standard deviation of a distribution divided by its mean, is a commonly used measure of horizontal equity (Odden and Picus 2004). In 1995, the coefficient of variation was 0.32 nationally, which was exceeded in seventeen states.

chapter three
Public Opinion and Americans' Commitment to Educational Spending

 According to Everett Ladd, "Americans are deeply committed to the enterprise of education. We say so every time we are asked, no matter how we are asked—and we put our money where our mouths are" (Ladd 1995, 22). Ladd points to government expenditures that have increased steadily since the 1960s and to public opinion polls showing that most Americans think that we ought to be spending more, rather than less, on public education.

We begin this chapter by reviewing forty years of public opinion polls in order to highlight the defining aspects of Americans' views about educational spending. In particular, we are interested in identifying and describing lines of political cleavage that form the foundation of local politics. We then want to see how these political cleavages combine with the demographic composition of each school district to produce varying commitments to public education across the roughly 10,000 unified school districts in the United States.

Political cleavages emerge because the history, economy, and culture of a nation give rise to groups that differ in their quality of life, their opportunities, or their values. In the United States, professionals differ from hourly workers, whites differ from blacks, and we see important political differences between inner-city and suburban dwellers, young and old, rich and poor—to note the most important social cleavages.

These social differences then lead to different political preferences. The differences may arise out of economic self-interest (e.g., home-owners may be less enthusiastic than renters about increases in local property tax rates) or from deeply held values associated with one's community, social class, or generation.

Our exploration of public opinion begins with the array of social divisions that span the nation: those based on age, race, ethnicity, socioeconomic status, parenthood, and homeownership. These demographic sources of opinion reflect how social position creates policy interests based on both the benefits of educational spending and how the costs of educational spending are borne unequally by different taxpayers.

In the subsequent section, we assess the "politics of place"—how region, type of community, and demographic composition give each school district a different level of support for education spending. We explain how we estimate local opinion in each of the nation's school districts and assess the validity of our measure.

Social Cleavages and the Demographic Sources of Opinion

Surprisingly, there is little previous research on social differences in support for education spending. Most of the published research is based on postelection polls concerning local bond referenda and other tax increases. However, exit polls and postelection surveys of referenda are poor guides to *public* opinion, because voter turnout may be quite low and not represent the public very well. Such exit polls may not even represent the opinions of registered voters, frequent voters, or voters in school board elections very well either. For example, MacManus (1997) notes that the demographic makeup of the voting electorate differed substantially between Tampa's 1995 (23 percent turnout) and 1996 (48 percent turnout) referenda. Tedin, Matland, and Weiher's (2001) study is based on a Houston bond referendum with an overall turnout rate of just 10 percent. Just as we would be skeptical of a sample survey with a response rate well under 50 percent, we must treat findings from exit polls and postelection surveys as suggestive at best. In addition, exit polls from bond or budget referenda are not applicable to the more than 3,500 school districts that have no referenda provisions at all.

Scholarly research based on nationally representative public opinion polls is virtually nonexistent, and there are only a handful of state-level (Bergstrom, Rubinfield, and Shapiro 1982) and community-level (Chew 1992) studies based on representative sample surveys.[1]

Although the number of analyses is limited, scholars tend to agree that support for educational spending is rooted in self-interest and values. We do not intend to delve into the intricacies of arguments concerning self-interest and values here. Although this is a controversial area of research (e.g., Sears and Citrin 1982; Sears and Funk 1990), the gist of the distinction is fairly straightforward. Self-interested citizens support specific policies because they (or their community) stand to benefit directly if the policy is enacted; others oppose policies because they will bear a direct cost and see few benefits. For example, most scholars agree that parents of school-age children have an immediate self interest in high educational spending while homeowners are likely to bear direct costs of spending increases in most communities in the United States (e.g., Preston 1984; Chew 1992; Tedin, Matland and Weiher 2001).

The notion of values is less clear-cut. Some economists refer to a "taste for education" that derives primarily from one's own education level and social class (e.g., Hoxby 1998). Presumably, well-educated, middle-class people (on average) place a higher value on education than others. This value translates into a willingness to pay higher taxes personally, pay more for houses in better school districts, and vote for politicians who share these views. In contrast, Moe describes a somewhat different value system when explaining "public school ideology": "Many Americans simply like the idea of a public school system. They see it as an expression of local democracy and a pillar of the local community, they admire the egalitarian principles on which it is based, [and] they think it deserves our commitment and support" (2001a, 87).

Sorting out the nature of such values is beyond the scope of our analysis. But for our purposes, the economists' "taste for education" approach points to educational attainment as the primary variable, whereas Moe's "ideological" perspective points to groups that have been consistently liberal and supportive of the Democratic Party—African Americans, lower-income groups, renters, and city dwellers—as the core population supporting educational spending. Consistent with these ideas, previous research based on both sample surveys and exit polls suggests that the important lines of cleavages are those based on age, race, parental status, homeownership, income, and education. We examine each of these in the next sections.

The Generation Gap

There is no more enduring political cleavage in America than the generation gap concerning school funding. National polls spanning nearly forty years show that older Americans are more likely to endorse lower spending on public schools and less likely to support spending increases. Table 3.1 reports results from polls fielded by four of the most prestigious academic and commercial research organizations in the United States: the Harris Poll, the Gallup Poll, the National Opinion Research Center at the University of Chicago, and the Center for Political Studies at the University of Michigan. The table provides the complete question wording for each poll and identifies the year, or span of years, that the question was asked. In each case, we report the percentage supporting higher spending and taxes among those under and over sixty-five years old and we calculate a generation gap. The results are easy to summarize: Seniors are 15 percent less supportive of educational spending than younger respondents.

The results show remarkable consistency and display a pattern that is virtually identical, even when question wording varies substantially. It seems not to matter whether the focus is on "schools here in this community," "the local public schools," or "the nation's educational system." It does not matter whether respondents were asked about "spending more money" or whether they would "vote to raise taxes." We see the same pattern in 1965 as we do in the 1970s and in the 1990s.

Published research leads to exactly the same conclusion. The generation gap is evident if the question asks about local spending (Chew 1992), federal spending (Vinovskis 1993), or spending in general with-

Table 3.1. For Nearly Forty Years, Older Citizens Have Been Less Supportive of Educational Spending Than Younger Citizens

Poll, Date	Question	Percent supporting higher spending or who think current spending is too low		
		Under 65	65 or older	Generation Gap
Harris Poll, March 1965	Do you feel too much money is being spent on public schools here in this community, too little money, or about the right amount of money?	29	13	16
Gallup / Phi Delta Kappa Polls, 1981–86	Suppose the local public schools said that they needed much more money. As you feel at this time, would you vote to raise taxes for this purpose, or would you vote against raising taxes for this purpose?	43	30	14
Harris Poll, August 1992	Even if it might mean higher taxes, would you favor spending more money on your community's public schools or would you favor spending less or about the same amount of money?	50	34	16
General Social Survey, 1973–85	Are we spending too much, too little, or about the right amount on improving the nation's education system?	58	41	17
General Social Survey, 1986–2002	Are we spending too much, too little, or about the right amount on improving the nation's education system?	73	58	15
National Election Studies, 1984–2000	Should federal spending on public schools be increased, decreased, or kept about the same?	69	53	15

out any reference to government (Ponza et al. 1988). Moreover, we find the generation gap in state polls in Alabama, Illinois, Florida, and New Jersey and in local polls in California's Orange County (Chew 1992), Long Beach (Knight Foundation 1999), and Aberdeen, South Dakota (Knight Foundation 1999, 2002). A small sample of these local and state polls is included in table 3.2, for illustration.

Table 3.2. Generation Gap Appears in a Wide Range of Local and State Polls

| Poll, Date | Question | Percent supporting higher spending or who think current spending is too low | | |
		Under 65	65 or older	Generation Gap
Knight Foundation Poll, Aberdeen, S.D., 1999	From what you know about how local tax money is spent, do you think the local government spends too much money on the public schools, too little money, or about the right amount?	49	19	30
Knight Foundation Poll, Long Beach, Calif., 1999	From what you know about how local tax money is spent, do you think the local government spends too much money on the public schools, too little money, or about the right amount?	64	51	13
Northern Illinois University, Illinois Policy Survey, November 1994	Now, I'd like to ask you some questions about spending by the state government in Springfield. Please bear in mind that eventually all government spending comes out of the taxes that you and other Illinois residents pay. . . . First, programs for public schools.	77	55	21
Rutgers / Eagleton Institute Poll of N.J. residents, March 1989	As you know, most of the money government spends comes from the taxes you and others pay. For each of the following, please tell me whether you think state and local government here in New Jersey should be spending more, less, or about the same as now: Public schools	63	51	12

In addition, the generation gap not only appears in opinion polls about *hypothetical* tax and spending increases but also in exit polls conducted during tax or bond referenda in such diverse locations as Houston (Tedin, Matland, and Weiher 2001), Tampa (MacManus 1997), and Michigan's Upper Peninsula (Brokaw, Gale, and Merz 1990).

In chapter 7, we will probe the source of the generation gap and its impact on local politics more deeply. However, for our purposes here, it is sufficient to simply note that the generation gap is large, enduring, and likely to create very different school politics for two otherwise similar school districts that differ substantially in the size of their populations of senior citizens.

In addition to age, scholars have identified four other demographic variables that consistently predict support and opposition to spending preferences for public schools: race, parenthood, homeownership, and educational attainment. We explore these and several related variables below.

Racial and Ethnic Differences

In the past fifty years, the public school systems of the nation have played a major role in preparing the first generation of African American lawyers, physicians, teachers, and other professionals—providing them with the tools to take advantage of new opportunities in higher education and the professions. Blacks are far less likely to be enrolled in private and parochial schools (Clotfelter 2004). More generally, blacks tend to be more liberal than whites, which leads us to expect greater support for government spending of all sorts.

Hispanics now make up more than 10 percent of the population and play an increasing role in state and local politics throughout the nation. Like African Americans, Hispanics are less likely than whites to be enrolled in private schools, and their schools are likely to spend relatively little per pupil. Conversely, language barriers for first- and second-generation Hispanics, more migration, and a greater incidence of seasonal employment have prevented Hispanics from matching blacks in high school graduation rates, college attendance, and entry into the professions.

Surprisingly, there is little systematic research on racial and ethnic differences in support for education spending. Bergstrom, Rubinfield, and Shapiro (1982) analyze a 1978 survey of Michigan residents and report that blacks are far more likely to support local spending increases. Additional research is based on postelection polls concerning local bond referenda and other tax increases. Tedin and his colleagues' survey of Houston voters (Tedin, Matland, and Weiher 2001) shows blacks far more supportive of a 1996 bond referendum than whites, with Hispanics generally supportive but less so than blacks. MacManus (1997) identifies blacks as strong supporters and Hispanics as opponents of a 1995 sales tax intended to benefit Tampa area schools but identifies Hispanics as supporters of a broader effort (funding a new football stadium as well as schools) just a year later.

Table 3.3 reports race differences in support for educational spending from five different national surveys. In every case, African Americans are more supportive of educational spending than whites, though the size of the gap is very large in the 1965 Harris Poll and very large in the lone study that specifically asks about spending by the federal government. More typically, the black/white gap is in the range of 5 to 8 percent. When we examine Hispanic identification, we find small and inconsistent results across the four national surveys that distinguished Hispanics from other respondents.

Parenthood

Parents of school-age children are likely to have a greater immediate self-interest in high-quality public schools than nonparents (an idea first articulated by Preston 1984 and elaborated by Chew 1992). Chew explains that nonparents realize little personal gain from investing in public schools and will tend to oppose tax and spending increases. "Their negative votes do not signify active opposition, but rather the greater salience of other priorities (such as transportation or health care) that manifest more relevance to their active self interest" (1992,

Table 3.3. African Americans Support Higher Spending than Whites and Hispanics

Poll, Date	Percent supporting higher spending or who think current spending is too low		
	Black/white differences		
	Blacks	Whites	Racial Gap
Harris Poll, March 1965	49	25	24
Gallup / Phi Delta Kappa Polls, 1981–86	49	40	9
Harris Poll, August 1992	51	47	5
General Social Survey, 1985–2002	76	68	8[i]
National Election Studies, 1984–2000	84	62	22
	Hispanics versus non-Hispanics		
	Hispanic	Not Hispanic	Ethnic Gap
Harris Poll, August 1992	40	49	–9
Gallup / Phi Delta Kappa Polls, 1985–86[a]	44	42	2
General Social Survey, 1985–2002	70	70	0
National Election Studies, 1984–2000	79	65	14

[a] Hispanic measure only in 1985 and 1986 surveys.

281). Chew's analysis of data from Orange County shows a strong effect of parenthood, with parents more than 50 percent more likely to say they would support a tax increase.

Tedin, Matland, and Weiher (2001) also treat parenthood as an indicator of self-interest and find that referendum voters with children in the Houston area public schools were 23 percent more likely to vote in favor of a school bond, even after controlling for more than twenty other variables. Our results are consistent with these community studies. We find modest gaps between parents and nonparents in all five national studies, with differences ranging between 5 and 11 percentage points (table 3.4).

Homeownership

Homeownership is also regarded as an indicator of immediate self-interest in the funding levels of public schools because most school

Table 3.4. Parents Support Higher Spending than Nonparents

	Percent supporting higher spending or who think current spending is too low		
Poll, Date	Parent[a]	Nonparent	Parenthood Gap
Harris Poll, March 1965	32	23	9
Gallup / Phi Delta Kappa Polls, 1981–86	47	38	9
Harris Poll, August 1992	51	46	5
General Social Survey, 1985–2002	72	67	6
National Election Studies, 1984–2000	69	59	11

[a] Operational definitions of "parent": Harris 1965, school-age children in household; GSS, children in household and respondent has child(ren) of own; PDK, parent of school-age children; Harris 1992, children under 18 in household; NES, children under 18 in household.

taxes come from property taxes. Of course, landlords will pass on property taxes to their tenants, but homeowners may be more likely to perceive costs to themselves and therefore be more likely to oppose funding increases. In the *Homevoter Hypothesis*, Fischel (2001a) argues that homeowners are the driving force in all local politics, determined through education, zoning, and other policies to maintain maximum value for their homes. This could lead them in many cases to support higher taxes for schools as a way of maintaining school quality and higher values for their homes. Here, all of our national data are consistent with the idea of short-term instrumental self-interest. We see that homeowners are less supportive of educational spending in every instance (table 3.5).

Socioeconomic Status

Scholars agree that education is a crucial predictor of support for educational spending. Those with advanced degrees may place a greater value on education both for their children and for the larger community, or they may have firsthand knowledge of how high-quality schools can make a difference in one's eventual economic attainment. Our five national polls show varying degrees of educational cleavage, but all lead to the conclusion that those with higher levels of education are more

Table 3.5. Renters Support Higher Spending than Homeowners

Poll, Date	Percent supporting higher spending or who think current spending is too low		
	Renter	Owner	Ownership Gap
Gallup / Phi Delta Kappa Polls, 1981–86	48	39	9
General Social Survey, 1985–2002	73	66	7
National Election Studies, 1984–2000	74	62	12

likely to support spending increases than those with less education. Table 3.6 summarizes these data by comparing those who earned a college degree with those who did not graduate from high school.

Income, the second major component of socioeconomic status, also is typically expected to be associated with support for educational spending, and four of our data sets reflect this. The impact of income is reversed in the National Election Study, which asks about *federal spending* and no doubt reflects the greater conservatism of affluent citizens.

However, the differences reported in table 3.7 are almost entirely spurious due to the prior effect of education. When we examine the effect of income among people with the same level of education, the impact of income disappears in the General Social Survey (GSS) and the 1965 and 1992 Harris Polls; it remains statistically significant but its

Table 3.6. Those with Higher Educational Attainment Support Higher Spending Than Those with Less Education

Poll, Date	Percent supporting higher spending or who think current spending is too low		
	College	Less than High School	Gap
Harris Poll, March 1965	44	21	23
Gallup / Phi Delta Kappa Polls, 1981–86	57	28	29
Harris Poll, August 1992	65	34	31
General Social Survey, 1985–2002	74	60	14
National Election Studies, 1984–2000	69	59	11

Table 3.7. Those with Higher Incomes Support Higher Spending Than Those with Less Income

Poll, Date	Percent supporting higher spending or who think current spending is too low		
	Highest	Lowest	Gap
Harris Poll, March 1965	32	19	13
Definition of highest and lowest categories	*Top 22*	*Bottom 13*	
Gallup / Phi Delta Kappa Polls, 1981–86	49	33	16
Definition of highest and lowest categories	*Top 23*	*Bottom 22*	
Harris Poll, August 1992	57	44	13
Definition of highest and lowest categories	*Top 20*	*Bottom 25*	
General Social Survey, 1985–2002	72	64	8
Definition of highest and lowest categories	*Top 20*	*Bottom 20*	
National Election Studies, 1984–2000	58	71	–13
Definition of highest and lowest categories	*Top 5*	*Bottom 16*	

effect is cut by roughly 60 percent in the Gallup / Phi Delta Kappa Poll. We will illustrate this in the next section, where we report regression analyses of data from the GSS. But the important lesson is that income does not have an independent impact on preferences, and thus we can think of it, in later chapters, as primarily an indicator of the ability to *afford* higher tax burdens and higher property values.

Underlying It All: A Commitment to Public Education

One of the remarkable features of the foregoing analyses is the similarity of results across very different surveys and question wordings. Consider the 1992 Harris Poll, a fifteen-minute telephone survey of 1,237 respondents, and the GSS, with 1985–2002 data based on over 26,000 face-to-face interviews that took over an hour to complete. As we noted above, the Harris Poll specifically mentions taxes and asks about spending money on "your community's public schools," whereas the GSS talks about costs in more general terms and focuses on the "nation's educational system." Although both surveys indicate that a majority of Americans want to spend more on education, the apparent level of support is much higher in the GSS. However, in both polls, seniors, whites, homeowners, high school dropouts, and the childless are less supportive than younger citizens, blacks, college graduates, and parents.

We come to the same conclusions when we examine surveys about state spending in Florida or Illinois, "state and local spending" in New Jersey, or local spending in Aberdeen, South Dakota, or Long Beach, California. We believe this means that all these questions are really tapping into something far more general than preferences for specific policies. Rather, the consistency across question wording, across time, and across place tells us that we are tapping into a more general *commitment to public education.* This is what Everett Ladd referred to when he wrote "Americans are deeply committed to the enterprise of education." (1995, 22), and this is the general commitment that economists refer to as a "taste for public education"—a taste that leads most Americans to support school bonds, endorse increased tax levies, elect school board officials willing to raise taxes, and pay higher prices for homes in neighborhoods with well-regarded public schools.

This is helpful to our enterprise because it means that communities endorsing high levels of spending on "the nation's educational system" should be the same communities that endorse increased taxes to pay for their "community's public schools." This allows us to utilize the GSS—which has by far the longest time series and the most detailed demographic information—as our primary means for ranking communities according to their commitment to public education. In other words, the GSS question on educational spending has face validity as an indicator of this broader commitment. As we will show later in this chapter, the GSS-based measure of public opinion also has high construct validity and predictive validity.

Social Cleavages: A Summary

In many respects, the politics of educational finance is no different from other policy controversies in the United States. Political divisions correspond to long-standing differences among generations, races, classes, and lifestyles. Whether these cleavages reflect instrumental self interest, long-standing values, or subcultures is an interesting and important question, but we need not answer that question in order to move ahead in our study of policy responsiveness. Whatever the "ultimate" causes, the vast body of opinion data suggests common patterns of educational politics throughout the nation. In almost every community, we are likely to see the most enthusiastic support for spending increases expressed by blacks, parents, and the well-educated; in almost every community, resistance to spending increases will come from older citizens, those with limited education, and homeowners.

Yet knowing the demographic composition of a community only provides the most general foundation for understanding that community's educational politics. As we will show throughout the book, the political institutions and organized groups in a community make an enormous difference in empowering certain demographic groups and limiting the influence of others. But before moving to institutions, we must move beyond demographics to understand "the politics of place"—how regional subcultures differ and how that helps us estimate the prevailing opinion in each school district.

The Politics of Place and Its Methodological Consequences

Local opinion is far more than the sum of the views of the various groups in a community, because every place has a local culture and every state has cultural tendencies as well. African Americans in California may have different views than those in Alabama, and senior citizens in Florida may have different preferences from those in Minnesota. State politics also influences how groups act in concert or oppose one another. Homeowners in small New England cities may have little in common with their neighbors who rent; but in other states they may work together. To estimate the prevailing opinion in each of the nation's unified school districts, we need to know more than the number of senior citizens, number of blacks, number of homeowners, and so on. We need to account for unique, state sources of opinion that political scientists lump under the catchall label of "political culture" (e.g., see Erikson, Wright, and McIver 1993, 47).

The fact that opinion depends on state contexts means that public opinion data have a "hierarchical" structure. Ordinary citizens—the respondents in all of our surveys—are clustered within states in three senses. First, ordinary citizens within a state culture are likely to be more similar to one another than they are to a group of comparable citizens in a neighboring state. This has some technical consequences for statistical analysis when we try to estimate how much different factors contribute to an individual's opinion on education spending—particularly that prediction errors (residuals) will be correlated within states.

Second, the prevailing culture in a state may lead citizens to be more liberal or conservative than we would expect based on their social background alone (Erikson, Wright, and McIver 1993). "Middle of the road" in New England might be more supportive of school spending than "middle of the road" in the Rocky Mountain region. In other words, citizens in each state begin with a different baseline political orientation. In regression analysis, this would translate into a different intercept for each state. Third, state cultures may enhance or diminish political cleavages. Black/white differences will be wider in some states than others, and it is inappropriate to assume (and use statistical models that implicitly assume) that various social gaps are the same everywhere.

To estimate the preferences of each major social group, while simultaneously addressing the three consequences of state clustering, we employ a technique called the hierarchical linear model (HLM), which is now one of the most commonly used methods in educational research and is becoming increasingly familiar to social scientists across many disciplines.

To examine the impact of demographics within state contexts, we use data from the GSS. As we have shown, the GSS captures all the important demographic cleavages and produces results quite similar to those of other surveys using different question variations. However, the GSS offers several enormous advantages compared with the other surveys. First, its sheer size allows us to examine very small subgroups—

for example, we can see if racial cleavages are wider in the Southeast than in New England. Second, the GSS allows us to restrict analysis to any particular time period that we may wish. As we will explain below, most of our independent variables were measured in 1990; by using GSSs from 1985 through 1994, we can develop an opinion measure that is also centered on 1990. Finally, the GSS allows us to generate reliable estimates for individual states and the effects of demographics within states.

Conversely, the GSS has one limitation, namely, that the sampling design is intended to be the nationally representative. Six states are not sampled at all (Hawaii, Idaho, Maine, Nebraska, Nevada, and New Mexico), and there is no guarantee that every state subsample will be representative of its corresponding population. This has not proven to be a major impediment to other scholars who have used the GSS to generate valid and reliable estimates of state policy opinion (Brace et al. 2002). Yet, as we will show below, this proves to be a particular problem with Wisconsin, two-thirds of whose residents live in metropolitan areas. In the GSS, however, only 36 percent of the sample live in metropolitan areas.

Who Supports Educational Spending?

The first step in understanding the "politics of place" is a comprehensive model predicting attitudes toward education spending. A multivariate model will tell us which demographic factors have a net influence on attitudes after controlling for all the others. Those variables that are spurious or otherwise accounted for by other measures need not be used in inferring the public opinion of each school district.

The statistical technique that we use in our comprehensive model is generally called a "hierarchical model" by education scholars and a "random coefficients model" by most political scientists and economists. In simple regression models, the effect of each variable is assumed to be the same everywhere. But with HLM, the effect of race, education, and all other variables can be different in each state. This will be crucial in our effort to estimate public opinion in each of the nation's 10,000 unified school districts. Our hierarchical regression model is reported in table A3.1 in appendix A, and the results confirm some, but not all, of the descriptive results presented in the first half of this chapter. We find that after controlling for all other factors, age has a very strong effect on spending preferences, with support for education spending dropping substantially as age increases beyond forty-five years old. Educational attainment also makes a substantial difference, with high school graduates almost 10 percent more likely than high school dropouts to endorse spending increases. Those with some college or a college degree are a bit more supportive, followed by those with advanced degrees. African Americans are more supportive of spending than whites, but Hispanics are no different from non-Hispanics. Though it may be to homeowners' long-term advantage to support higher spending for schools, the multivariate model confirms our earlier finding that homeowners are significantly less supportive than renters of spending more for education. But neither parenthood nor income has the effect we saw in simple cross-tabulations, and size of place has an impact only when we compare central cities with suburbs and smaller locales within states.

The results in table A3.1 resemble those of a traditional regression analysis. But recall that the effect of each variable can vary from state to state. Table A3.1 actually reports only the average effect of each demographic factor on individuals' support for education spending. For example, the average black/white gap is 0.084, with African Americans about 8 percent more likely to think current spending is too low (after accounting for education and all other demographic factors). Yet, we estimate the black/white gap to be 0.13 in Pennsylvania, Missouri, and Ohio (all political swing states that have large rural populations, many small cities, and large African American populations concentrated in their largest central cities). In contrast, we estimate the smallest black/white gaps (less than 0.03) in Arizona and California—two states with multiracial political competition. It is not our point to explain these state-by-state differences here. Rather, we accept these state-to-state differences as reflecting real differences in racial cleavages from place to place, and we utilize these to infer public opinion in each school district. We explain how we do so in the next section.

Small Polity Inference

In this section, we describe in general terms the method that allows us to rank all American school districts from least to most committed to financing the public schools. Greater detail is included in appendix A.

The study of state and local opinion has two traditional approaches. The oldest is the so-called simulation approach (Pool, Abelson, and Popkin 1965; Weber et al. 1972). Some also call this the "demographic" approach because it is based entirely on demographic predictors of public opinion. The second approach is generally referred to as the "aggregation" method because researchers combine many different public opinion polls and aggregate individual poll respondents into states, creating, for example, the equivalent of fifty state polls using the same method. This allows researchers to garner large sample sizes even for small areas (Erikson, Wright, and McIver 1993; Brace et al. 2002). The large sample sizes allow researchers to take advantage of relatively small margins of error and make inferences about public opinion in states or communities.

Using Demographics to "Simulate" Public Opinion

The demographic approach to opinion estimation was pioneered by Pool, Abelson, and Popkin (1965) in their capacity as consultants to John F. Kennedy's 1960 presidential campaign. Ronald Weber and his colleagues (Weber and Shaffer 1972; Weber et al. 1972) adapted the method and were the first to employ it to study the linkage between constituency opinion and policy outputs. In the simulation approach, scholars employ national polls to calculate the policy preferences of specific "types" of citizens. For example, the GSS data suggest that 71 percent of white, college-educated homeowners think current educational spending levels are too low. In contrast, 88 percent of black renters with a graduate degree think spending is too low. In the simulation approach, we would assume that black renters with a college degree were the same everywhere and by determining how many black renters with a college degree lived in a state or town, and determining how many people of all other "types," we could estimate the opinion in that state or community.

The Limits of Demographics and the Method of Aggregating Opinion Polls

Some scholars continue to use the simulation approach (e.g., Moffitt, Ribar, and Wilhelm 1998; Werner 1998). However, the method was overtaken by *estimation by aggregation* with the publication of Erikson, Wright, and McIver's *Statehouse Democracy* (1993). They began with partisanship and ideology data from 167,460 interviews from thirteen years of CBS / *New York Times* polls. They then divided the data by state so that each state had its own "poll" with enough respondents to yield an acceptable margin of error. This approach has been extended most recently by Brace and colleagues (2002), who used the GSS's thirty years of replications to build state-level measures of public opinion on nine policies.

Erikson, Wright, and McIver demonstrated that after controlling for a comprehensive set of demographic variables, state of residence explained considerable variance in individual opinion. State cultures were not simply the sum of demographic characteristics but also functions of history and political institutions not easily measured in sample surveys. In short, the simulation method—which relied entirely on demographics—must yield flawed estimates.

Unfortunately, it would be impossible to use the method of estimation by aggregation to estimate the opinions for 10,000 school districts. For one thing, no national poll identifies the school district of each participant in the poll. And even if they did, we would require more than 10 million survey respondents to generate reliable opinion estimates for each school district.

Exploiting the Strengths of Each Approach

Small polity inference is a technique to infer public opinion for communities, or polities, so small that they may not show up at all in traditional public opinion polls. Small polity inference combines the best elements of each of the traditional approaches. Above, we described how hierarchical models differ from traditional regression models. One important consequence is that they allow us to calculate a baseline opinion for each state. This is similar to the aggregation method, and we can address the major weakness of the simulation approach: ignoring state culture. However, we can use the demographic composition of a district to distinguish it from otherwise similar districts in the same state. This takes advantage of the main strength of the simulation approach. But we improve on this further, because hierarchical models allow us to capture how the differences between homeowners and renters, between blacks and whites, and all other cleavages differ from place to place. Unlike the early efforts to simulate opinion, we need not assume that these political divisions are the same everywhere.

If we know the opinions of each "type" of citizen and know how many of each type are in each school district, it is a simple matter of calculating a weighted average of the preferences of each type of citizen. The technical details describing how we do this are contained in appendix A.

Spending Preferences within and across the States

Our measure of spending preferences reflects the percentage of adults who think school spending is too low in each of the nation's 10,000 school districts and is standardized to have a mean of zero and a standard deviation equal to 1. The measure can range from –3 (virtually no one in the district thinks spending is too low) to +3 (almost everyone feels that spending is too low). The range of opinion within any particular state, however, is much narrower. We show this in figure 3.1 for the forty-four states included in the GSS. The states are arrayed in order of their median preference value, and the distribution of the data within each state is represented by the ends of boxes (the 25th and

Figure 3.1. Variation in Public Opinion toward School Spending within and across States, 1995

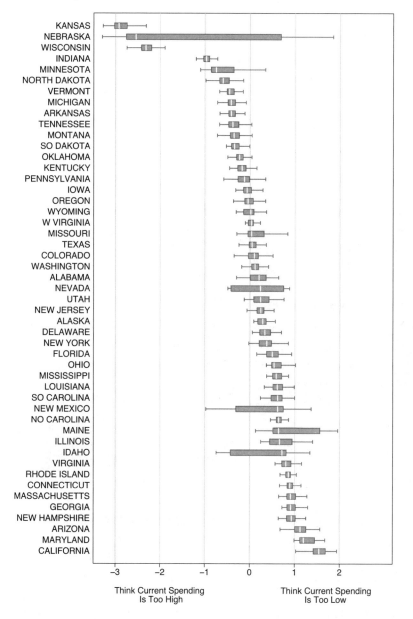

Source: Authors' measure of local commitment to education spending, based on an analysis of General Social Survey, 1985–94, and U.S. Census, Special Tabulation; see chapter 3 and appendix A for details.

75th percentiles) and the whiskers (the last values before outliers). Most of the variation is across states, but there is significant within-state variation as well.

Two of the states are problematic. Wisconsin, as we noted above, undersamples urban areas; the consequence is easily seen in figure 3.1: Wisconsin appears more conservative than we might expect. Similarly, the GSS sampling of Kansas also underrepresents urban areas, and the median opinion in Kansas is roughly 3 standard deviations more conservative than that of the typical state. Kansas is a conservative state by most accounts (e.g., Erikson, Wright, and McIver 1993). Nevertheless, this degree of conservatism seems implausible. We elected to drop Wisconsin and Kansas from all analyses using this variable. As a result, all our analyses of policy responsiveness in this book are based on the remaining forty-two states.

Is Our Measure Valid?

A crucial test for any measure is whether or not it is valid; that is, does the indicator really measure what we want it to? A common and intuitive way to assess the validity of our measure of opinion is to examine how much it is correlated with actual spending outcomes. For example, we can ask how well our measure of spending preferences (over the period 1985 to 1994) predicts 1995 per-pupil spending within states. The results (purely descriptive and without controlling for other factors that might influence spending) are presented in figure 3.2.[2]

The results show that our measure of local opinion is strongly associated with local spending levels. Of course, this is exactly the relationship we hope to study—and we expect it to be higher and lower under specific conditions. So any particular slope could reflect the impact of institutions on policy responsiveness more than reflecting the validity of the measure.

We therefore sought to assess the validity of our measure in three different ways. If our measure is valid, it should meet three criteria. First, it should be related to concepts that are theoretically linked to support for public schools (i.e., convergent validity). Second, it should be highly correlated with outcomes of measurement approaches that

Figure 3.2. Local Opinion toward School Spending Has a Strong and Positive Impact on Local Spending Levels

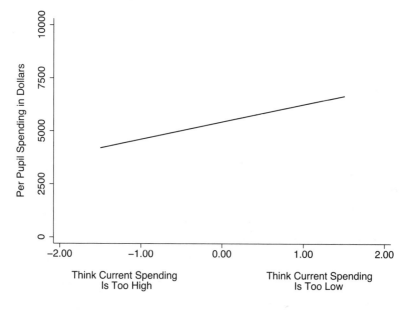

Think Current Spending Is Too High   Think Current Spending Is Too Low

Sources: Authors' measure of local commitment to education spending; 1995 Local Education Agency Finance Survey, distributed by National Center for Educational Statistics.

are generally accepted as valid (criterion validity). Third, it should *not* be highly correlated with measures of theoretically similar, but distinct, concepts (discriminant validity).

Convergent Validity

Economists have long viewed school spending in terms of one's "taste" for educational spending. Though we believe that preferences for increased spending by the schools should be reflected in higher actual spending, economists also expect that these tastes will be reflected in higher housing values (Hoxby 1998; Fischel 2001a). If our measure is a valid indicator of spending preferences, it should also predict high housing values—high relative to citizen resources. Figure 3.3 shows the results of this examination. The vertical axis is median housing value

Figure 3.3. Local Opinion toward School Spending Is a Powerful Predictor of Local Housing Values, After Controlling for Local Median Income

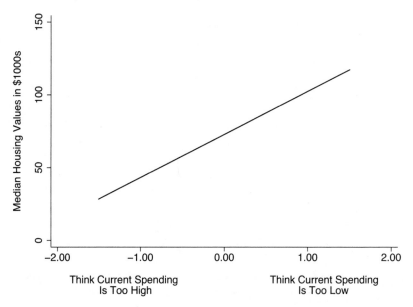

Source: Authors' measure of local commitment to education spending, based on an analysis of General Social Survey, 1985–94, and U.S. Census, Special Tabulation; see chapter 3 and appendix A for details.

(in thousands of dollars), and the horizontal axis is our measure of public opinion. The regression line represents the effect of public opinion on housing values after controlling for local median income. This allows us to see if a high commitment to education is associated with high housing prices for districts that do not differ in income.

The results show that our opinion measure has a strong, positive, and significant relationship with housing values. A school district scoring 1 point above average on our opinion measure would have home values about $29,000 higher than districts with only average opinion. We should point out that while few states have school districts where opinion spans the full range of possible values across the country, in most states the most liberal districts do differ from the most conservative by about a full point.

Criterion Validity

We can also assess validity from the perspective of aggregation, the widely accepted method for assessing state-level public opinion. If we apply small polity inference and we use the method of aggregation on the same set of cases, how closely are they correlated? Correlation coefficients of zero would indicate that the measures are completely unrelated, and a coefficient of exactly 1 would indicate that the aggregation and small polity inference produce "parallel" measures of the same concept. We cannot use the aggregation method on school districts, but we can use small polity inference to generate an opinion estimate for each state. When we do so, we find that the two alternative approaches are correlated at a level of 0.67. Thus the measures are highly, but not perfectly, correlated.

Of course, both approaches have sources of error. Small polity inference imposes a uniform opinion on everyone within a certain type in the same state—even as we know that the opinions of sixty-five-year-old white citizens in Fort Lauderdale might differ from sixty-five-year-old white citizens in Miami. We hope that such errors are random and small and will cancel each other out across the 10,000 districts in our study. Aggregation also has random error due to small sample sizes in each state. Indeed, if we exclude states with fewer than 100 GSS respondents, the correlation increases to 0.75. Another way to account for small sample and random error is to "correct" the correlation coefficient for known levels of random error. We can assess the degree of random error in the aggregation measure, and when we account for this, we get a corrected correlation of 0.84—an indicator of nearly parallel measures.[3] Thus, at the state level, the two methods produce very similar results, with at least some of the difference due to random error. So if aggregation is valid, the small polity inference must be valid as well.

We should note that as units of analysis become more internally heterogeneous and exhibit less interunit variation in demographics, small polity inference is likely to perform poorly. Thus, small polity inference should not perform as well at the state level as at the district level. Thus, the very high correlation between methods at the state level may be taken as a lower bound of the validity of the method.

Discriminant Validity

Finally, valid measures should *not* be highly correlated with distinct but closely related constructs, such as general ideology. To test this, we again use state average of spending preferences for the forty-two states in our analysis and see how closely it is correlated with Erikson, Wright, and McIver's (1993) widely used measure of state policy liberalism. As we would expect, there is a positive relationship between the two, with liberal publics being somewhat more supportive of educational spending (after all, commitment to public education spending should be a component of overall liberalism). But the relationship is weak, with a correlation of only 0.24. If our measure of commitment to public schools were simply a parallel measure of general liberalism, the correlation would be expected to be much closer to 1.0. This test therefore provides additional evidence that our measure taps into a distinct concept.

In this section, we described not only how we employed small polity inference (with more details contained in appendix A), but we also assessed the validity of the measure in several independent tests. The original question we used taps a broad dimension of commitment to public education and has strong face validity. The measure predicts not only educational spending (as it should if institutions effectively translate public preferences into policy) but also predicts housing values, as required by most economic approaches to school spending. It produces state rankings that are almost identical to those produced by aggregation, but the measure is not highly correlated with general ideology. In short, we feel our measure provides a reasonable estimate of local preferences for school spending.

Conclusion

Our analyses have shown that Everett Ladd was correct: Most Americans think that educational spending is too low and are willing to endure higher taxes if the revenue benefits the public schools. However, this does not mean that a majority in a particular community will endorse *any* tax increase. A school board can easily propose a tax increase so large that even the most liberal citizens will oppose it. Thus whenever school spending comes before the public's attention, there is likely to be a coalition favoring the increase and a coalition that is opposed.

Our analysis shows that these coalitions are formed in large part on the basis of personal and economic characteristics. Not all tax increases are controversial. But when they are, young voters, African Americans, parents, and those with a high level of educational attainment themselves are likely to support it. Older Americans, homeowners, and those with lower levels of educational attainment are likely to be in the opposition. We are confident in these characterizations because attitudes toward education spending vary systematically across these major social cleavages, have persisted across time, and are revealed not only in national surveys but in many state and community polls as well. The cleavages appear across a range of survey methods, and across a very wide variety of question wordings.

If individual characteristics are important, then communities with different types of individuals must necessarily differ from one another. We take advantage of this fact in order to develop a school-district-level measure of commitment to public education spending.

Our measure of local public opinion allows us to rank all American school districts from those least supportive of public school spending to those with the greatest commitment to spending more in order to improve the public schools. Of course, commitment in the absence of financial resources is not sufficient to transform a local public school system, and economic resources play the major role in distinguishing the high-spending from low-spending schools within a particular state. Thus when we examine the impact of public opinion on actual policy outcomes, we must account for the ability to pay. As a result, all remaining statistical models in this book include "controls" for local property values, the median income in the community, and population size, which can create economies of scale for large school districts.

Our preliminary, descriptive model (in figure 3.2) shows that public opinion matters—a lot. Districts scoring high on our measure of commitment spend hundreds of dollars more for each child enrolled.

Most of this goes into higher salaries and benefits for teachers and support staff. After salaries, most of the remainder goes into school libraries, computers, and enhancing the quality of the physical space in which students learn. Thus local public opinion makes a big difference in determining the level of resources that communities actually devote to their schools.

Yet, it would be naive to assume that public preferences are always translated into actual policies. The ability of the public to have its voice matter depends on a myriad of institutional and community characteristics. In the next chapter, we begin to identify the conditions under which policy responsiveness is enhanced or retarded by political institutions that were originally *intended* to distance school boards from their publics. We will see that some of these institutions amplify the voice of the average citizen while others seem to marginalize the role of public opinion in the policymaking process.

Notes

1. Several economists have attempted to estimate the demographic influences of *demand functions* for education spending, but this is somewhat different than estimating public opinion because estimating demand functions for it requires the estimation of specific monetary costs to individuals. Because education spending can be increased by reductions in other government programs (e.g., prisons, roads, or parks) the demand function approach does not lend itself to analyses that cut across different types of governments that may have rather different methods for funding public schools.

2. The model is $SPENDING_{ik} = b_{0k} + b_{1k} OPINION + u_{ik}$, where b_{1k} is the effect of opinion in state k. The average value of b_{1k} is 818. This means that on average, across all states, a 1-point increase in our opinion measure increases spending per pupil by $818.

3. We use the O'Brien ratio generalizability method to assess the reliability of the aggregation measure (Jones and Norrander 1996). By this criterion, the aggregation method has a reliability of 0.64, and the corrected correlation is 0.84.

chapter four

Direct Democracy, Indirect Democracy, and Policy Responsiveness

To what extent does policy responsiveness depend on ordinary citizens being closely involved in the formulation of tax and spending policies? Political institutions at all levels of the federal system have been designed with very different answers to this question. In his *Federalist Paper 10*, James Madison made a strong case against direct popular control, particularly in small polities. Larger republican governments are best, he argued, because representative bodies filter public views while a large and diverse public sphere hinders the development of majority factions.

But, as Morone (1998, 6) forcefully argues, a "democratic wish" also runs through American political history. This "wish" values direct participation premised on the un-Madisonian idea that "people agree with one another." The institutional legacy of the colonists and Progressives is built upon this premise: Direct democratic control, and in the Progressive case scientific administration as well, can fulfill these common interests. In this chapter, we consider how effectively this legacy—realized in the colonial town meeting, the Progressive independent school district, and the varieties of referendum arrangements—links the public with policy outputs.

Fiscal Independence and Policy Responsiveness

The most visible legacy of the Progressives' "one best system" is the organization of American public schools into *independent* government entities, responsible for both the financing and administration of schools under their jurisdiction. A smaller number are *dependent*, where budgetary and other decisions rest in the hands of another overlapping or coterminous level of government.

In many large cities—New York and Baltimore, for example—schools are dependent on the municipal government; whereas southern states, with their strong traditions of county government, are more likely to make their school districts dependent on counties. In these cities and counties, school financing and school governance are a major responsibility of mayors and council members, who must weigh educational spending against other services such as law enforcement, fire protection, and public parks.

New England has historically placed power and control in its towns, and we see that many education policies continue to be made by town governments or even multiple town governments when a single school district encompasses several. Finally, a very small number of districts are dependent upon state governments. Aside from state-dependent districts in Alaska, state dependency today arises most frequently when a troubled district is temporarily taken over by its state government.[1] Table 4.1 captures some of the variety of possibilities for how a district may be dependent upon other governments and how this varies by region.[2]

Progressive reformers opposed all forms of dependency and advocated independent school districts as a means of distancing boards from the corrupt partisan politics of turn-of-the-century cities. This "buffering" from "local control" (Tyack and Cuban 1995) was intended to allow independent school board members "to suppress public participation" (McDermott 1999, 80) and separate "school policymaking from poorer neighborhoods and school government from general-purpose government" (McDermott 1999, 43–44). The Progressives believed that this independence would lead school boards to represent the public interest rather than either particular constituencies or the interests of partisan politicians.

Like the council–manager form of local or city government but with even greater penetration throughout the country, independent school districts headed by professional superintendents and fairly small school

Table 4.1. Independent and the Various Types of Dependent School Districts, Unified (K–12) Districts Only, by Region, 1992

Region	Independent School District	Dependent on:			
		State	Municipal County	Township	Total
New England	196	0	0	92	274	562
Mid-Atlantic / Great Lakes	2,904	2	23	19	3	2,951
Central	3,224	0	0	1	0	3,225
South	1,965	0	301	59	0	2,325
Pacific/Mountain	1,280	20	10	22	0	1,332
Total	9,569	22	334	193	277	10,395

boards persist as a distinct and impressive legacy of Progressive institutional innovation. Today, 95 percent of all districts—representing about 85 percent of all students—are fiscally independent, and 90 percent of these boards operate with nine or fewer elected members (with five being the modal size). Without the need to incorporate other local or city concerns into their calculations, these school boards were expected to act with an ethos of doing "what is best for the schools" rather than through the more political calculus of partisan officeholders. By restricting themselves to the responsibility of making good school policy, they would not have to respond to demands and concerns about other aspects of community politics. The separation of school boards from the public through independence reflects well what Morone (1998, 112) sees as a "paradox" in the Progressive agenda: Independent school boards bypass "institutions that had distorted public sentiment" so that government "would be simultaneously returned to the people and placed beyond them, in the hands of experts" (p. 98).

We cannot evaluate whether or not policy outcomes in independent school districts "better" represent the schools or some abstract community interest. But we can assess their impact on spending decisions and how closely these decisions align with public preferences. First, we can see whether or not dependent districts have different spending patterns than independent ones. To do this, we want to show the estimated

spending level of dependent and independent districts in the same state
that are otherwise identical in their tax base (income and housing values) and other factors that can influence spending levels. To assess this,
we estimated a multiple regression model that *controlled* for all these factors. For this and the subsequent three chapters, we will provide details
of our regression models in the chapter's appendix. Each appendix not
only includes the tables containing the regression results but also gives
a brief narrative explaining the analyses, the methodological decisions
we made, and (where appropriate) a critical guide to interpreting the results. Major findings are displayed graphically, with the key results for
economic and institutional effects on spending *levels* illustrated by vertical bar graphs. The major findings concerning policy responsiveness
are illustrated either by line graphs or horizontal bar graphs.

Figure 4.1 is a bar graph showing the impact of fiscal independence
on per-pupil spending and is based on the regression model reported
in table A4.1 in appendix B. The graph shows that when we hold all the
economic, tax, and state factors constant (at their average values), dependent districts are expected to spend $5,878 and independent ones
$5,388, a difference of $490 per pupil.

Why should dependent districts spend more than independent
ones? If anything, we might initially expect otherwise. In dependent districts, the school budget is one among many items. In an independent
district, residents and board members consider what is "good for the
kids" or "the schools" in isolation from, for example, what is best for
the seniors, commuters, or major employers. In a dependent district,
conversely, school advocates must argue for *a piece of the pie* as well as
the size of the pie. Bryan (2004) shows that in some Vermont communities, where all schools are dependent on town governments, school
spending advocates try to break school budget discussions off into separate meetings to keep certain populations from having a say in school
affairs. Spending will be protected, these advocates of school spending
argue, if they can look at it in isolation.

Yet in dependent districts, "log rolling" (I'll vote for your pet project if you vote for mine) may allow for higher spending outcomes than

Figure 4.1. Dependent School Districts Spend More Per Pupil Than Independent School Districts

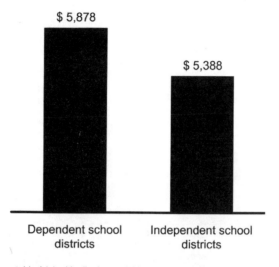

Source: Based on table A4.1 with all other variables at their mean.

in independent districts where log rolling is not possible. There may be advantages to having more people or interests argue for the overall size of the pie. We contend, however, that though there may be theories of institutional decision making that can explain this, the stronger explanation lies in policy responsiveness. As the Progressives intended, decisions in independent districts are not as responsive to public opinion as in dependent districts.

To show this, we need to estimate the impact of public opinion on public policy—what we call "policy responsiveness"—for all independent districts and all dependent districts (while accounting for their tax bases and all of our other "control variables"). As we noted above, this is assessed by *statistical* interactions; the model testing the appropriate interaction is reported in table A4.2 in appendix B, and the key results are illustrated in the line graph displayed in figure 4.2. The solid line shows the degree of policy responsiveness in fiscally independent districts. By any measure, the independent districts are responsive because

Figure 4.2. Policy Responsiveness Is Greater in Dependent School Districts
Than in Independent Districts

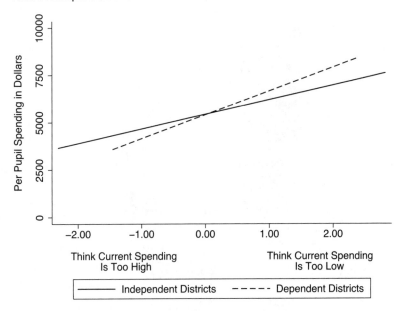

Source: Based on table A4.2 with all other variables at their mean.

a one-unit (1 standard deviation) increase in public support for school spending results in an additional $726 per child. But the steeper slope of the dashed line shows that dependent districts are considerably more responsive than independent ones. Because dependent districts are more supportive of spending increases, this responsiveness leads to higher levels of spending. People in independent districts may be getting less than they ask for; at the very least, people in dependent districts are getting closer to what they ask for.

Citizen Budget Power in American School Districts

It would, however, be premature to conclude from the analysis in the previous section that all independent school districts are equally responsive to public opinion. There are more than 8,500 independent, unified school districts in forty-nine states, and they operate under a variety of rules and procedures that allow their publics either more or less ability to vote, approve, or participate in final budgetary decisions. It would be equally premature to conclude that all dependent districts are equally responsive. Though there is less variation in this smaller universe of districts, we also find here a theoretically interesting mix of ways for the public to indicate its approval of school budgets. Presumably, school board officials in these institutional contexts both understand and respond differently to district preferences.

We summarize these citizen budget powers by region for unified (K–12) independent and dependent districts in table 4.2. In over 2,700 independent school districts (and nearly 400 dependent districts), school boards are relatively insulated from public control over final budgetary outcomes. In these districts, which include all the districts of fourteen states (Alabama, California, Florida, Illinois, Indiana, Iowa, Montana, Nebraska, Nevada, New Mexico, Pennsylvania, South Carolina, Utah, and Wyoming) along with districts in other states, school boards are not unlike other representative bodies. Though board members in most of these states are elected by citizens of the district—we will see in chapter 5 that not all districts use elections—the board determines spending and taxing levels on instructional expenses without the need to gain public approval through a formal vote at any point in the process.[3] Citizens' direct budgetary powers are therefore most limited in these districts.

But even in those districts lacking direct citizen input into annual budget decisions, we frequently find a requirement for public approval of any bonds floated to finance public projects—usually large capital ones. These referenda requirements were established in the late 1800s and early 1900s by Progressives as a protection against large and excessive public debt (Wirt and Kirst 1997; Howards 1967). Although originally motivated by a desire to limit large-scale borrowing for major capital expenditures, referenda are currently used in the vast majority of independent districts to gain public approval for the funding of school *instructional* expenses as well. In a referendum, voters approve

Table 4.2. Citizen Budget Powers by Fiscal Independence and Region

District Type	No Citizen Budget Power	Referendum for Tax Increases over a Certain Amount	Referendum for All Tax Increases	Referendum on Full Budget	Town Meeting
Independent					
New England	41	29	0	44	187
Mid-Atlantic /					
Great Lakes	962	1,135	70	784	0
Central	913	1,190	1,205	0	0
South	285	1,295	378	0	0
Pacific/Mountain	538	533	248	0	0
Total	2,739	4,182	1,901	828	187
Dependent					
New England	58	39	0	2	166
Mid-Atlantic /					
Great Lakes	39	0	0	0	0
Central	0	0	0	0	0
South	256	0	119	0	0
Pacific/Mountain	53	0	0	0	0
Total	406	39	119	2	166

measures offered by the legislature or local government (Eule 1990; Magleby 1984; Cronin 1989). By consulting various sources and speaking with state school board associations, education departments, superintendents, and education experts, we were able to code referendum powers for all districts in the early 1990s.[4]

There are several conditions under which districts using referenda must offer them to voters. The most expansive arrangement is employed by most of New York's and New Jersey's independent districts, as well dozens scattered across towns in four New England states (including many that previously used town meetings). In this arrangement, budget referenda must be offered each year, with expenditures and tax revenues clearly stated and presented to the public for an up or down vote.[5] Though these are generally low-turnout elections, they can be high-profile affairs, with editorials in local newspapers, letters to the editor, telephone banks, and campaign literature. And though most pass, a nontrivial number do not (Muir and Schneider 1999).

A larger number of independent districts, as well as 119 county-dependent districts in North Carolina, require a referendum only when the board of education calls for an increase in school taxes. In some districts, this is a straightforward requirement for tax increases of any amount. The largest number of school districts, spread across all regions other than the Mid-Atlantic, operates under provisions requiring a referendum for tax increases over a certain amount. Laws vary widely among the fifteen states in this category. In Kansas, school districts a referendum can be triggered by the protests to tax increases of 5 percent of registered voters; in Georgia, local districts may levy up to 20 mills without voter approval; and in Kentucky, a referendum is required when funds go above a certain state-set level. There are as many different rules within this category as there are states.

The final category of citizen power is unique to New England and includes the more than 300 districts that, so far as we can tell, were still holding town meetings in the mid-1990s. The town meeting is, in the words of Frank Bryan—who has studied them more than anyone else— the only "real democracy" where people make "decisions that matter" in a face-to-face setting (2004, xi). About half the districts in this category are dependent upon their towns, which means the school budget is determined at the same town meeting as the town budgets; others use separate financial meetings. But in each case budget approval is given only by those present. And though the idea of a town meeting is that all residents are together developing public policy, in reality the budget is developed, written, and presented to the public by the school board working with the school superintendent.

The town meeting is "not to be confused with direct plebiscites" (Bryan 2004, 4) like the referendum, and indeed it is an old system of governance that predates the American constitution. Town meetings have withstood Progressive attack, and the difficulties associated with holding multi-hour-long meetings with a more suburbanized, heterogeneous, time-challenged public. But it is a system in flux—town meetings are hardly on the rise—and our ability to accurately determine exactly which districts held town meetings in the 1990s was at times frustrating. In Maine, for example, there are sixty-four school administrative districts (SADs). These were established in the late 1950s to bring the school districts of several communities together into one. They originally used town meetings, common to Maine communities, where the residents of the SAD would meet as a town and determine the budget. Over time, however, SADs have moved away from town meetings toward a referendum on the full budget. We never could establish when these shifts occurred in which SADs, so we could not code these communities. In New Hampshire a 1995 law (SB2) allowed school districts to abandon their town meeting, and many have.[6] Fortunately, in this case, we know that, prior to the law, districts did use the town meeting. And we know that in Vermont many towns have moved toward a budget referendum (Bryan 2004), but we believe we were able to figure out what each was doing in the mid-1990s by contacting school districts directly. In the end, through exhaustive e-mailing and World Wide Web searches, we could code nearly all New England districts as to whether they were using town meetings in the 1990s and if not how budgets were approved.[7]

Citizen Budget Power and Policy Responsiveness

Which of these systems should most enhance or retard policy responsiveness? Some of the strongest theoretical guidance on this question comes from studies of the initiative, a purer form of direct democracy, and these suggest that the initiative should draw policy outcomes closer to district preferences. Indeed, Wirt and Kirst argue that budget referenda link "the individual citizen to the school in a direct and intimate way that is unparalleled for other major public policies" (1997, 115). But the initiative is not the same as the referendum, and town meetings are different altogether. Perhaps that is why Wirt and Kirst also note that budget referenda "fall short" (1997) on linking citizen demands to public policies, although the literature on the importance of the types of rules we saw in table 4.2 is actually quite limited and difficult to generalize.[8]

The Initiative and Referendum

The initiative differs from the referendum in that it allows voters "to replace representative government altogether" (Cain and Miller 2001, 37; Eule 1990) by directly proposing laws and policies rather than simply approving those offered by the legislative body.[9] Academic research on the initiative has largely settled on two important conclusions that offer a good starting place for our investigation of referenda and town meetings. The first is that governments will spend less when the initiative is available; the second is that they spend less because that is what the public wants. As Matsusaka finds in a comparison of thirty years of spending by state and local governments, the initiative "inhibits government spending" because elected representatives will, if left to their own devices, "spend more than the median voter wishes" (1995, 590; see also Farnham 1990; Steunenberg 1992; Pommerehne 1978).

For public choice scholars, the initiative creates a system that better approximates a true "political market" (Romer, Rosenthal, and Munley 1992), where outcomes settle on preferences of the median voter. Because voters have less say, governing institutions introduce "noise" that weakens the link between the preference of the median voter and actual policy outcomes (Farnham 1990).[10] And because the initiative shifts the balance of power away from the governing body, "the community's fiscal behavior in equilibrium reflects the outcomes that are most preferred by the median voter" (Turnbull and Mitias 1999, 119). Indeed, even if the initiative is not used at a particular time for a particular measure, its very threat causes governments to act in ways more consistent with voter preferences (Matsusaka 1995, 2001; Gerber 1996a, 1999; Arceneaux 2002).

The "noise" introduced by representative legislatures could be random. This would mean that the relationship between spending and opinion may be greater in districts with direct democracy than in those without, but the level of spending would be essentially the same in both.

But many direct democracy scholars, and supporters, go further, arguing that the noise is systematic and leads to higher spending than the public prefers. This is because log rolling and other incentives lead legislatures to be "budget maximizers." Thus, direct democracy not only should be expected to increase responsiveness but also to lower tax and spending levels.

The referendum is also one among other important "constraint[s] on local government spending" (Courant, Gramlich, and Rubinfield 1979, 806). In at least one important way, however, the referendum is different, and the policymaking body is in a stronger position vis-à-vis the public. In a referendum, the legislature or policymaking body has certain advantages in realizing its preferences because it sets the agenda by acting first and putting proposals before the voters; in an initiative situation, voters theoretically go first (Steunenberg 1992; Romer and Rosenthal 1982). Gerber (1996a), however, shows that this distinction is not as great as it seems at first because when the initiative is available legislatures will *anticipate* public preferences and go first.[11]

Of course, the relevant comparison in American school districts is not between the referendum and initiative but between school districts where residents have more complete referendum rights and those where they have fewer or none. We could find only one head-to-head test between districts that used the referendum and those that did not, and the results in that study were inconclusive (Megdal 1983). But it seems to us that a board operating in an environment where the public has more restricted referendum powers is more insulated and under less pressure to take public opinion into account than in districts where citizens enjoy more expansive referendum rights. School board directors facing a referendum for approval need to propose budgets that can pass, and they understand full well that there are implications if they do not.[12] If a budget referendum fails in New Jersey, for example, the budget decision is taken away from the board and citizens and given to the larger municipality.[13] In New York, a failed budget referendum requires the adoption of a state-mandated contingency budget limited by the spending of the previous year or a new, smaller budget in a new vote. And in most locales, a failure to win approval for a substantial tax increase means paying the opportunity cost of forgoing a more modest tax increase that might have passed.

A referendum should lead school boards to pay more attention to public preferences, but this is important only if their preferences are actually distinct from those of the public. Because most median voter models are constructed without any, or at best rough, measures of community preferences (Lascher et al. 1996), this is a problematic assumption. Zax (1989), for example, contends that voters actually want to spend more than their legislators and that those ordinary citizens are the true budget maximizers. Our thorough review of public opinion in chapter 3 provides substantial evidence for this assertion. Stevens and Mason argue similarly that school boards may not be the maximizers legislators are assumed to be because board members are "expected to keep property tax down" and "budget maximization is an unlikely objective" (1996, 259). Other work reaches similar conclusions consistent with the position that school boards see themselves as protecting the public and taxpayers against the spending preferences of professional administrators.[14] So even if the referendum does, in its various guises, keep outcomes closer to the median (Stevens and Mason 1996), school districts with greater referendum opportunities may spend more, not less, than those with fewer opportunities.

There is, however, an even more critical problem that arises with the median voter model as it has been used in initiative and referendum studies. That is the implicit assumption that when we talk about the median voter whose preferences are realized through direct democracy we are actually talking about the preferences of the community at large.[15] But this assumption is inconsistent with what we know about these elections. Direct democracy clearly leads to different outcomes than when a decision is made through the legislative process (Gerber 1996b); this does not mean that the preferences of the community at large have been better realized through direct democracy. In fact, we should be cautious.

Voting turnout is low, especially in local elections, and there is an additional drop-off in voting for initiatives and referendum. Those who do vote are likely to be unrepresentative of the community at large (Magleby 1984; Cronin 1989; Wirt and Kirst 1997), while some organized interests have advantages in direct democracy campaigns (Gerber 1996a, 1996b). "Initiatives," therefore, "are an imperfect reflection of public desires" (Lascher, Hagen, and Rochlin 1996, 772) and may be "systematically including or excluding different groups from the policy process" (Gerber 1996b, 283). That is why studies at the state level that directly measure preferences are mixed on whether the referendum allows for outcomes closer to those of the community's preferences (Gerber 1996a; Matsusaka 2001; Lascher, Hagen, and Rochlin 1996).

Much the same can be said of the town meeting, where turnout is also likely to be low and participation limited, especially in larger towns (Bryan 2004). Further, those with lower levels of education and weaker speaking skills may feel excluded and unable to participate in town meetings (Mansbridge 1980). It is interesting that Bryan, throughout his fine book *Real Democracy* (2004) about New England communities, never makes the argument that town meetings will enhance responsiveness. Rather, his emphasis is on the quality of the participatory experience, the dialogue, the educative value, all important to democracy but hardly necessary to responsiveness. So though we may expect higher levels of responsiveness in smaller communities that use the town meeting, based on nothing else then their greater homogeneity and findings from town meeting research (Bryan 2004), the same problems with participation that taint the referendum may be true in these communities as well.

Because we can measure citizen preferences on school spending, we can overcome one of the vexing problems facing those who try to assess the effects of direct democracy on fiscal outcomes. But we are cognizant of those organized or coherent in their interests that might pull spending away from preferences of the median in the community. Initiatives have been particularly important to antitax campaigns (Magleby 1984; Cronin 1989), so we might expect antitax interests to take advantage of referenda opportunities. School referenda are generally seen as a means for people to register discontent with their schools (Wirt and Kirst 1997). But there is even more to it because school referenda are, in many communities, the only opportunity that citizens have to regularly vote on governmental taxing and spending. They are, therefore, to Guttman "by far the most effective and obvious means by which citizens can register their decision to slow down government spending and taxation" (1987, 141–42).

All these would lead us to expect that direct democracy and town meetings pull outcomes below the preferences of the median voter. But antitax interests and those antagonistic toward government are not the only ones that show up for school referenda elections. If they were, budgets would never pass. Parents are an important interest in school politics (Salisbury 1980), and school boards work with parent groups to make sure supporters turn out to pass school budgets (e.g., Mac-Manus 1997). We expect teacher unions do as well, and we devote chapter 7 to examining their influence.

Dependent Districts

We showed above that dependent school districts were more responsive to public opinion than fiscally independent districts. Of the roughly 700 dependent K–12 school districts, just under one-fifth are those in which school budgets are determined by elected city councils (across eight states) and a third are by county governments (in Maryland, Tennessee, and Virginia). About 25 percent are New England communities using colonial town meetings, and 16 percent are North Carolina counties. We examine each type of dependent district to see if some are more responsive than others. Whenever we examine four or more groups simultaneously, we report policy responsiveness in horizontal bar graphs, rather than line graphs. Longer bars correspond to steeper slopes, and the length of each bar tells us how much more spending is associated by comparing an average district with an identical one that is one unit more liberal in its public opinion (figure 4.3).

Figure 4.3. Policy Responsiveness in Dependent Districts Varies According to Citizen Budget Power

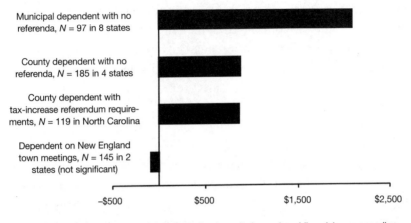

Note: The horizontal bars represent the effect of a one-unit change in public opinion on spending levels, in dollars per pupil, with all other variables at their mean.
Source: Based on table A4.3.

The results are striking. Only New England towns among all the dependent school districts are not responsive at all. Conversely, school districts dependent on municipalities—the very sorts of school districts initially attacked by Progressives as controlled by political parties and urban machines—are the most responsive of all. These districts are not, we should note, restricted to big-city schools, although this category does include some of these; along with the New York, Buffalo, and Providence school districts are smaller ones in Tennessee, Virginia, and New Hampshire. A one-unit change in opinion within these ninety-seven school districts spread out among eight states leads to a dramatic change in spending, and shows that the Progressives' concern with using independent districts to insulate school boards from their publics was effective. The county-dependent districts are also responsive to their publics, with those in North Carolina, where citizens must approve all tax increases, more responsive than those in four other mostly southern states. However, in order to probe the impact of referenda

Figure 4.4. Policy Responsiveness in Independent Districts Varies According to Citizen Budget Power

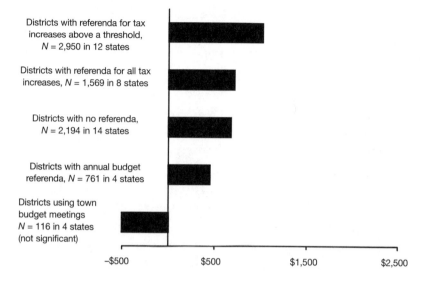

Note: The horizontal bars represent the effect of a one-unit change in public opinion on spending levels, in dollars per pupil, with all other variables at their mean.
Source: Based on table A4.4.

rights more generally, we now turn to the far more numerous independent school districts.

Independent School Districts

Most school districts in the United States are fiscally independent and detached from the local governments that are responsible for everything other than education in their respective communities. As we showed in table 4.2, these independent districts encompass the full range of ways that citizens might influence the budget process. As in the case of dependent districts, we examine each type of citizen access arrangement separately. Figure 4.4 shows the impact of a one-unit change in opinion for each of the five types of districts. As in figure 4.3, they are aligned from least to most responsive.

The results show enormous variation in policy responsiveness across the varieties of citizen access arrangements. The slope of opinion is not statistically significant—essentially zero—in the case of districts using town meetings. Whether school districts are dependent upon other units of government or independent of them, town meetings do nothing to enhance responsiveness.

We see that the most responsive districts are those using a particular form of referendum where tax increases are put for a vote only when taxes are scheduled to rise above a certain amount. These districts are more than twice as responsive as those using general budget referenda and significantly more responsive than districts without any referendum requirements at all or those that put all tax increases up for a vote. There must be something in the dynamics when a board attempts to develop budgets that allow increases of a certain amount without approval—and where the goal must clearly be to avoid a vote altogether—that allows school boards to settle on outcomes closest to citizen preferences.

Conclusion: Citizen Budgetary Power and Spending Levels

It is apparent from the analysis above that citizens participate in the local school budget process in a wide variety of ways. Most states have followed the Progressive prescription to separate policymaking from the public and routine politics by organizing the majority of their school districts independently from other local governments. But a nontrivial number remain dependent on other units of government, and these are among the most responsive to public opinion. Some school districts in New England retain the colonial practice of conducting business through town meetings. Despite their celebration as "true democracies" (Bryan 2004), they come up short in at least one test of any democracy: They do not appear to be a particularly responsive form of government. Whether compared with traditional republican forms of representative democracy or different types of referenda, the town meeting is consistently the least responsive form of government.

Progressives also advocated referenda of various types, and the general message about these is mixed. Theoretically, we might expect referenda to operate like initiatives and promote greater responsiveness, and this is the argument that is generally made about their use at the state and local levels. Conversely, the initiative and referenda do have different roots—the referendum is much more in the Progressive tradition than is the initiative, which is more in the Populist tradition—so we should not necessarily be surprised to find that referenda do not have the same responsiveness properties as we might expect from initiatives. After all, the Progressives were more interested in checking legislatures than they were in responsiveness, whereas the Populists "wanted to substitute direct popular control for representative government" (Cain and Miller 2001, 37).

Public choice scholars argue that high levels of responsiveness and spending levels are related because responsiveness will place a check on the spending proclivities of legislators. This may well have been the original intent of referenda, as we noted above: Wirt and Kirst (1997, 114) argue that school referenda were "the handiwork of conservatives" seeking to keep property taxes and debt low. But do these tools of direct democracy achieve this goal? And do they do it by being more responsive? The actual picture is complex. We have already seen that districts using referenda are responsive, but some are not much more responsive than districts that do not use referenda at all (not including town meetings). To see differences in spending levels across types of citizen access—as opposed to responsiveness—we report average spending levels by each form of citizen power (adjusted to account for differing housing values across the forms). Table 4.3 shows that among the five types, the system with the most access (annual budget referenda and town meetings) not only has relatively low levels of responsiveness but also the highest levels of spending. Among the three most common systems, spending levels are essentially identical.

In the following chapter, we follow up on the strong responsiveness found in districts that provide no citizen budgetary power at all by considering the role elections play in translating public preferences into

Table 4.3. In Independent School Districts, Overall Spending Levels Do Not Vary Systematically with the Amount of Citizen Access to the Budget Process

Types of Independent School Districts	Effect of a One-unit Change in Opinion (dollars)[a]	Average Spending Level (dollars)[b]
Districts with referenda for tax increases above a specific threshold, N = 2,950 in 12 states	1,017	5,061
Districts with referenda for all tax increases, N = 1,569 in 8 states	703	4,941
Districts with no referenda, N = 2,194 in 14 states	674	5,268
Districts with annual budget referenda, N = 761 in 4 states	446	7,793
Districts using town budget meetings, N = 116 in 4 states	(579)	5,723

[a] Effect of opinion is from table A4.4.

[b] Average spending level after holding housing values constant.

concrete policy decisions. Referenda and other forms of direct democracy are only one way in which public officials, policy outcomes, and the public are linked together. As we will see, there is as much variety in the means of selecting school board members as there is in providing citizen access.

Notes

1. Most state-dependent districts are found in Alaska, where nineteen of fifty districts are state dependent. State dependency is different from state financing. E.g., in Alaska some localities are responsible for as little as 1 percent of all revenues, whereas in others it is as high as 56 percent. But decisions about taxing rest with the state government.

2. Throughout chapters 4 and 5, states are categorized into the following regions. *New England:* Maine, Vermont, New Hampshire, Massachusetts, Connecticut, and Rhode Island. *Middle Atlantic / Great Lakes:* New Jersey, New York, Pennsylvania, Michigan, Ohio, Illinois, Delaware, Maryland, and West Virginia. *Central:* Wisconsin, Indiana, Minnesota, Iowa, Missouri, North Dakota, South Dakota, Nebraska, Kansas, Oklahoma, and Kentucky. *South:* Virginia, North Carolina, South Carolina, Georgia, Florida, Alabama, Mississippi, Arkansas, Louisiana, Texas, and Ten-

nessee. *Pacific/Mountain:* Washington, Oregon, California, Alaska, Hawaii, Utah, Wyoming, Idaho, Montana, Colorado, Arizona, Nevada, and New Mexico.

3. Districts in this category do not exclude the public; they just do not need to gain formal approval through the vote. Many of these districts, if not most, have citizen advisory committees, open board meetings, and separate budget meetings.

4. Our primary source was the *Public School Finance Programs of the United States and Canada, 1993–1994*, vols. 1 and 2 (Gold, Smith, and Lawton 1995), hereafter PSF. We checked this against the U.S. Census of Governments for cases in which PSF was ambiguous or the information was missing. Finally, when we were still uncertain we consulted experts in the state, at either a state university or the state education department. In most cases, we consulted the expert who had written the appropriate chapter in the PSF. If this was not possible, we consulted the finance office of the state education department.

5. As of 1997, all independent districts in New York used referenda, but prior to then fifty-seven districts in cities of under 125,000 people where city lines coincided with school district boundaries school budgets were not subject to a referendum. We also include in this category New Jersey districts operating under a system of second questions, which are additional requests for expenditures above the state-imposed budget cap, as well as New England school districts that operate under the Australian ballot system. In these New England districts, budgets are discussed at a town meeting but voted on in separate, free-standing elections. Many New Hampshire communities switched to an Australian ballot system or other systems after 1995 (Hall and Knapp 2000); the information in table 4.3 is valid for the early to middle 1990s.

6. Senate Bill 2 (SB2) created RSA 40:13, which provides a mechanism for voters to replace the traditional open town and school district meetings with an official ballot process. If voters in a town or school district adopt SB2, subsequent years' budgets will be discussed and amended in the open meeting but are only voted upon by ballot on the town election day.

7. We are grateful for the tenacity of Marcie Seiler and Beth Klemick in tracking these down.

8. There is a fairly substantial literature on bond referenda, most prominently the work by Tedin, Matland, and Weiher (2001). But these are different from the budget referenda identified above and are not focused on the issue of responsiveness. On school budget referenda in particular, see Megdal (1983), Inman (1978), and more recently Stevens and Mason (1996) along with Romer, Rosenthal, and Munley (1992). With the exception of Megdal, however, this work does not compare districts that offer more with districts with fewer referendum rights.

9. Some see the initiative as more closely related to the Populists than the Progressives (Cain and Miller 2001), because they do not see the Progressives as motivated to advance democracy (McDermott 1999). Morone (1998), conversely, does recognize the referendum in the tradition of direct democracy.

10. This noise is introduced because governments generally and legislators in particular are assumed to be "log-rolling" budget maximizers who deliver particularized benefits for their own political interests (Matsusaka 1993; Steunenberg 1992; Weingast, Shepsle, and Johnsen 1981).

11. In a direct comparison between an initiative and referendum procedure, however, the legislature's greater agenda-setting power should allow for outcomes closer to their preferences than the public's. There is some evidence to support this. E.g., when Farnham (1990) looked at the use of initiative and referendum in state and cities he found that use of the referendum actually *increased* expenditures.

12. This follows from Romer, Rosenthal, and Munley's (1992) argument that board members incorporate their knowledge of where the median voter stands relative to the budget that will be adopted if the referendum fails.

13. We thank Mike Yaple of the New Jersey School Boards Association for pointing this threat out to us.

14. Inman (1978) looked at school districts on Long Island, where the referendum is used, and found either that outcomes were consistent with the preferences of the median voter or that spending was slightly lower than those presumed preferred by the median. But his measures of the median voter's preferences are assumed from demographics.

15. E.g., Turnbull and Mitias (1999, 119) characterize the "median voter model" as a method of aggregating individual voter-taxpayer demands to arrive at some notion of *community* demand" (emphasis added here and in other quotations in this note). Fischell (2001a, 87) characterizes "the median-voter model of politics" as the "social-science name for *majority rule*" and characterizes Bowen's (1943) initial hypothesis about the median voter as saying that under majority rule the "*householder* who had the median income" would get the public services and taxes s/he demanded.

chapter five

Voting Rights, Electoral Systems, and Policy Responsiveness

Most school board elections are low-key affairs often held apart from more exciting and competitive national and state elections. If there is no controversial issue on the immediate agenda, there will likely be little campaigning and little discussion of the issues. Participation is usually minimal, turnout low, and the content of the campaign trivial unless the public is particularly dissatisfied by a recent policy decision. Candidates often run unopposed and unaffiliated with political parties (McDermott 1999). One could easily conclude that school board elections are not very important.

Can that be? After all, our theory of school board responsiveness requires links between board members and the public. As we saw in chapter 4, though most states offer some meaningful degree of referendum power, only a small number of states allow residents to vote directly on school budgets. Policy responsiveness varies according to the type of referendum system but does not depend on direct democracy. Public opinion is clearly related to spending outcomes in the many dependent and independent districts that have no referenda of any kind. We show that throughout most of the nation the method of choosing school board members is important to how public opinion is translated into policy decisions. We do so by showing how electoral and selection rules shape who is chosen, and we explore whether this has implications for how well board decisions reflect community preferences.

Consider, for example, the Hinds County school district in Mississippi, which serves more than 5,000 students in eleven schools. In 1987 the U.S. Census Bureau conducted a census of all governments in the country, including school districts. This Census of Governments showed that Hinds County used a five-member elected school board. Yet, despite the fact that 44 percent of the school district's 32,000 residents were black, all its school board members were white. Five years later, the Census Bureau returned to conduct what was, unfortunately, the last census of government officials done by the bureau. Between 1987 and 1992, Hinds County changed the way it elected school board officials, dividing the county into electoral wards. By 1992, two black school board members had been elected, so that the board was now 40 percent African American, closely matching the population of the district.

We find similar stories across the country. Black membership on the school board doubled from 14 to 30 percent in the Kakohee, Illinois, district, which is 30 percent African American; they also switched from electing members at-large to electing them through wards. In New Jersey, one black school member was elected to the nine-member board in the 12-percent-black Palmyra Boro school district after they switched to ward elections.

Of course, when choosing from among 10,000 school districts, it is easy to find three conforming to a particular pattern. But as we will show, these three cases are excellent illustrations of the more general trend: New ways of electing representatives led to greater racial parity on American school boards. Conversely, many districts still use appointment powers first developed by Progressives to bypass elections altogether. Our analysis in this chapter addresses the evolving politics of electoral system reform beginning with the Progressive Era and continuing through the consequences of the civil rights movement. As in the previous chapter, we show that institutional designs developed in previous periods of reform continue to shape responsiveness in American school districts.

Descriptive Representation and Policy Responsiveness

The landmark Voting Rights Act of 1965 contributed to greater black enfranchisement and larger numbers of elected African American officials throughout American local governments (Welch 1990; Davidson and Grofman 1994a).[1] As a result, African Americans have achieved greater *descriptive* (or *passive*) representation, by which we mean that local governing bodies look more like the communities they serve. As Mansbridge explains, descriptive representation means that "representatives are . . . in some sense typical of the larger class of persons whom they represent" (1999, 629; see also Pitkin 1967). In contrast, policy responsiveness is a measure of *substantive representation*: whether elected officials *act* in accord with the wishes of the citizens they represent.

In this chapter, we look at how school districts select their boards. As we will see, most school board officials are elected, and a smaller number are appointed by other local or state elected officials. We show, first, that the method of selection has a major impact on the level of descriptive representation and, second, that descriptive representation can be an important pathway toward greater policy responsiveness (Mansbridge 1999; Stewart, England, and Meier 1989). We have already seen, for example, that blacks have a distinct preference to spend more on education than do whites. These preferences, however, may just as well be represented by liberal white school board members as black ones. In other words, it somewhat begs our central question to focus solely on the election of African Americans; instead, our concern is whether descriptive representation and different electoral systems foster greater policy responsiveness.

Our analysis is framed by the politics of race. The discriminatory impact of different schemes for choosing public officials has been a persistent theme in American political history. We will see in this chapter, for example, that between 1987 and 1992 hundreds of districts changed their electoral systems because of concerns about racial discrimination and underrepresentation. Our data allow us to look not only across American school districts but also at those that changed. This enables us to speak to debates about which types of electoral systems are most fair and most democratic. We expect electoral systems that allow for greater racial representation will be, overall, more representative of their communities and therefore more responsive as well. We are not interested, therefore, in black preferences for school spending but in whether systems that allow for greater representation for blacks will be more responsive to the whole community.

We first discuss the importance and roots of electoral systems in American local government—in particular, the discriminatory potential of at-large elections. We then offer an empirical assessment of descriptive representation on school boards, consider whether changes in electoral systems systematically promoted greater descriptive representation, and see how these contribute to policy responsiveness. Our findings are in one sense quite consistent with other research on local political electoral systems—we find, for example, that ward-based elections enhance black representation whereas at-large elections can retard it. But they are also counterintuitive—we will show, for example, that the most responsive systems may not use elections at all.

The Voting Rights Act and Discriminatory Electoral Systems

To Chandler Davidson and Bernard Grofman (1994a), the 1965 Voting Right Act spurred a "Quiet Revolution" in how elections are conducted. The act targeted areas of American political life that directly or indirectly disenfranchised black voters and diluted black political power. Electoral systems were of particular interest because of how they could be manipulated to systematically underrepresent minorities. The at-large elections used by many local governments and most American school districts received extensive scrutiny. They were a particular target when the act was amended in 1982 and when the Supreme Court established tests for at-large districts in the North Carolina case of *Thornburg v. Gingles* (1986). Yet for all the changes, Davidson and Grofman (1994b) note that the quiet revolution was an incomplete one, leaving many districts unchanged and producing a patchwork of civil rights reforms overlaid on the wide variety of arrangements inherited from the Progressive Era.

At-Large and Ward Elections

Single-member ward elections are often associated with the political machines of the nineteenth century, but they were actually widely used throughout the South and West as well (Davidson and Grofman 1994b). Under a ward-based system, candidates run for a specific seat representing a small geographic area within the political jurisdiction. The residents of the ward may only vote for candidates running for that ward's seat. Ward elections are especially valuable to a geographically concentrated minority. Although not a majority across the entire city, county, or school district, an ethnic or racial group concentrated within a ward can influence that ward's election, field its own candidates, and therefore gain representation on the governing body.

The same logic is often applied to the construction of majority-minority districts in the U.S. House of Representatives; where a statewide minority of black voters spread out over all House districts there could be, and often were in the South, no elected black representatives. But where concentrated as a majority or near majority in a congressional district, blacks are assured some measure of descriptive representation within the state congressional delegation.

Ward elections were critical to the maintenance of nineteenth-century political machines. Ethnic and working-class candidates could campaign among their friends and neighbors within homogenous electoral wards. This type of campaigning is more difficult in at-large elections, where each candidate must run in the entire jurisdiction. Because Progressive reformers felt that "the enfranchisement of recent immigrants was a major factor in corrupt city governments" (Davidson and Korbel 1981, 985), at-large elections were promoted as one of several reforms to undermine machines by taking "government out of the hands of neighborhood and ethnic leaders" (Davidson and Korbell 1981, 987).[2] They understood that "spatially concentrated groups of voters are 'swamped,' 'absorbed,' 'submerged,' or 'diluted'" (Scarrow 1999, 558) by at-large voting. Further, because there are many names on the ballot from throughout the political jurisdiction, candidates must "campaign over a wide area, and consequently are often complete strangers to most of the electorate" (p. 560). At-large elections put a premium on name recognition or candidates with enough resources to become known across a large area; and they advantage more educated and sophisticated voters, who must navigate ballots with unfamiliar names and, usually, without party labels.

Welch and Bledsoe (1988) write that the reformers were looking for "better people"; Banfield and Wilson refer to these new officeholders as "public-regarding" men (1965) who would "depoliticize local government" and put "as much distance as possible between the people and their local government" (Welch and Bledsoe 1988, 55; also see McDermott 1999). Reformers were relatively successful in these efforts. Political machines in many cities were effectively weakened as at-large elections reduced the representation of residents on lower socioeconomic levels (Welch and Bledsoe 1988).

Yet the effects of at-large elections were most pernicious in the South, where "Progressivism coincided with the peak of racial reaction" (Davidson and Korbel 1981, 987).[3] Because the disenfranchisement of immigrants was central to the political strategy of northern Progressives, southern Progressives made "the race issue their chief stock-in-trade and were among the principal advocates of disenfranchisement" (Davidson and Korbell 1981, 988). At-large elections spread throughout the post-Progressive period, especially in the South, as elites came to appreciate their value in diluting the black vote just as African Americans were becoming more enfranchised and acquiring political power (Davidson and Grofman 1994b; Davidson and Korbell 1981).

At-large elections contributed to low rates of electoral success for African American candidates through the 1970s.[4] With the passage of the Voting Rights Act of 1965, subsequent extensions, and court decisions, city after city "dropped at-large electoral systems and replaced them with either districts or mixed" systems (Welch 1990, 1050). As those districts with the most discriminatory track records were challenged and reformed, the gap in black representation between at-large and ward elections was effectively reduced in the 1980s (Welch 1990).[5]

Electing School Boards

Meier and his colleagues have noted that Progressive efforts to reform local governments were more successful in school districts than in American cities (Meier, Stewart, and England 1989; Banfield and Wilson 1965). Table 5.1, based on our analysis of data from the Census of Governments, shows that nearly 80 percent of school boards used at-large elections in 1987.[6] There are significant regional patterns, however.[7] Many western and southern school districts had, by 1987, already faced court challenges to their use of at-large elections and were in some cases operating under court supervision, so we see somewhat less frequent use of at-large elections in these regions than in the North.[8]

But though many of the largest southern districts, along with those having the most egregious discriminatory voting systems, had already shifted to wards by the late 1980s, the "quiet revolution" was far from over in the "hundreds of smaller towns where the effects of the Voting Rights Act as a means to prevent minority vote dilution have not yet been felt" (Davidson and Grofman 1994b, 386). This finding in Davidson and Grofman's comprehensive study of voting rights in eight southern states has particular significance for the consideration of American school districts (which were not their main focus). Most school districts are relatively small. One-quarter of all school districts in the country have populations below 3,000, and only 2 percent have more than 100,000 residents. Even in the South, where school districts tend to be larger, the median district is only 9,566 people.

Figure 5.1 compares the use of ward-based elections in school districts of different sizes. We again look separately at southern and nonsouthern states. As we expected, in the late 1980s, smaller southern districts were much less likely to be using ward-based elections (and therefore more likely to be using at-large elections) than larger ones. In the quartile of smallest school districts (measured by population), for example, fewer than 3 percent used ward elections compared with 20 percent in the largest. Looked at the other way (not shown), nearly 96 percent of the smallest districts used at-large elections in 1987). Outside

Table 5.1. Methods of School Board Selection, by Region, 1987 (percent)

Region	District	At-large	Mixed	Appointed	No. of Cases
New England	7	88	3	1	560
Mid-Atlantic /					
Great Lakes	6	93	0	1	2,947
Central	9	77	13	1	3,245
South	13	69	6	12	2,309
Pacific Mountain	27	70	3	0	1,262
Total	11	79	6	4	10,323

Note: Each region's percentages total 100% except for New England, which is less than 100% due to rounding.

the South, there is virtually no size pattern at all. Though we knew from other research that smaller *municipal* governments were less likely than larger ones to have switched to district elections in the wake of the Voting Rights Act (Welch 1990), we now know that the same was true of school districts.

Figure 5.1 also shows an increase throughout the country and in districts of all sizes in the proportion of school districts using ward elections between 1987 and 1992.[9] In the South, where the shift to ward elections had already begun prior to 1987, change was most dramatic in smaller school districts: The proportion of lowest-quartile southern districts using ward elections increased sevenfold (from 2.9 to 20.3 percent) and fivefold among the second-quartile districts, and it doubled among the third quartile and increased by less than that in the largest districts.

Overall, more than 3,000 unified school districts changed how their boards were chosen in the five-year period between 1987 and 1992. We believe this occurred because 1982 amendments to the Voting Rights Act spurred many southern municipalities to switch to ward elections (Davidson and Grofman 1994b). These 1982 amendments to section 2 of the act prohibited voting practices that resulted in discrimination *regardless of intent* (McDonald 1992; Davidson and Grofman 1994b). This meant that plaintiffs needed only to show that a voting procedure "resulted in members of the protected classes having less opportunity than other members for the electorate to participate in the political process and to elect representatives of their choice" (quoted in Davidson 1994, 35).

Figure 5.1. In the South, Small School Districts Are Less Likely to Use Wards; Outside the South, There Is No Relationship between Size and the Use of Ward-Based Elections

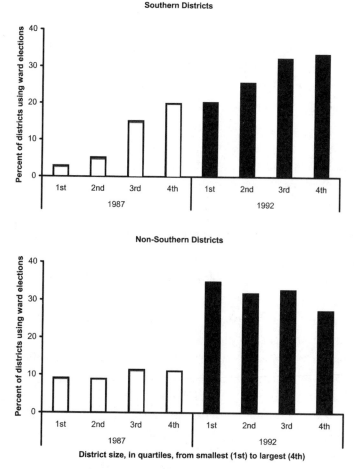

Source: U.S. Census of Governments, 1987 and 1992.

But of perhaps even greater importance, hinted at in Davidson and Grofman's study of the South but missed because much of their data analysis stops in 1989, was the Supreme Court's interpretation of these in the 1986 case of *Thornburgh v. Gingles.*[10] *Gingles* put a spotlight directly on at-large elections by establishing a clear three-part test for de-

termining when they were discriminatory. Whether or not this specifically led to school district changes we cannot say for certain, although
it was referenced in at least thirty state court cases that we have been
able to identify. After *Gingles* was announced, 90 percent of section 2
challenges to southern municipal at-large elections were successful
(Davidson and Grofman 1994b). *Gingles* contributed to a substantial
increase in litigation and settlements in anticipation of litigation (Mc-
Donald 1992; Davidson and Grofman 1994b), so hundreds of political
jurisdictions accepted the "inevitable and adopted less dilutive forms
of elections" (Davidson and Grofman 1994b, 383). Our data suggest
that hundreds of school districts, too, "having seen the handwriting on
the wall" (Davidson and Grofman 1994a, 5), switched from at-large to
district elections. We explore the consequences of this below.

Black Representation on American School Boards

As we documented in the previous sections, at-large elections are
used throughout the country to select American school board members. Their impact on the composition of American school boards has
been similar to their impact on other units of local government. Wirt
and Kirst argue, for example, that the initial Progressive shift to at-large
elections in the early part of the twentieth century led to the disappear-
ance of working-class school board members while "middle-class members dominated everywhere" (1997, 102). Welch and Bledsoe note a
similar finding for American cities and local governments. At-large elections, argues McDermott, "*prevent* boards of education from constitut-
ing microcosms of the public or representing the full range of opinion
in the community" (McDermott 1999, 83; italics in original).

At-large elections have also contributed to the underrepresentation
of African Americans on American school boards (Meier and England
1984; Welch and Karnig 1978; Robinson, England, and Meier 1985) by
diluting black votes. But the Voting Rights Act was intended to alter the
balance of power by outlawing those electoral systems that dampened
African American candidates' electoral prospects in racially polarized

voting environments. Linda Meggers, the director of Georgia's state reapportionment office, called the post-*Gingles* shift to district voting "the most revolutionary change in Georgia since the Civil War. You're having a whole new distribution of power" (quoted in McDonald, Binford, and Johnson 1994, 84).

The extent to which changes in electoral systems have actually shifted the balance of power by electing minorities to American school boards is not well understood (Stewart, England, and Meier 1989). So far as we can tell, there is no exhaustive accounting of descriptive representation on school boards in the United States. Much of the extant research focuses on the nation's largest school systems, none takes into account the sorts of changes in black representation identified by Welch (1990), and the one study that includes both urban and rural districts (Arrington and Watts 1990) is of a single state and reaches some different conclusions than those reached by those studying larger urban districts.[11] In the next section, we provide the first comprehensive empirical assessment of how electoral systems have an impact on minority representation on school boards, and how the change from one system to another alters minority representation.

The Election of African Americans to School Boards

There are two ways to assess descriptive representation. The *ratio method* is widely used to give a representation score to each school district, whereas the *regression method* provides an assessment of districts overall or of those in a particular region, time, or electoral type.

The ratio method compares the percentage of blacks on the governing body—in this case, the school board—with the percentage of blacks in the community. This ratio increased substantially between 1987 and 1992, from 0.40 in southern states in 1987 to 0.55 in 1992, and from 0.42 outside the South in 1987 to 0.83 by 1992. All the ratios are less than 1.0, showing that blacks are generally underrepresented; the score of 0.83 indicates that blacks were close to parity by 1992 outside the South.[12] This ratio measure offers an individual score for every community, and we make use of a variant of this in the analysis below. However, the measure scores all districts without a black representative as zero, irrespective of whether there are any blacks in the community or not (Engstrom and McDonald 1981). This makes it improper to treat low scores as indicators of racial injustice.

Engstrom and McDonald (1981) have developed a method of measuring minority representation that overcomes this problem (Bullock 1994) and easily accommodates the inclusion of all communities, although many researchers choose to restrict the analysis to cities with minority populations of at least 10 or 15 percent (e.g., Robinson, England, and Meier 1985). Their *regression method* describes the relationship between the proportion of blacks in the population and the proportion on the school board based upon a simple regression model. Their method gives us two important pieces of information vital to understanding the nature of descriptive representation in a school district or other jurisdiction. First, we can determine how the black presence in the community translates into black seats; for example, whether a 10 percent increase in black residents in the community translates into a comparable 10 percent increase in the proportion of blacks on the school board. Second, we can determine whether there is a threshold level above which blacks need a presence in the community to have any representation on the board at all.[13]

We use the regression method to evaluate descriptive representation in five types of school districts: those that used at-large elections in 1987 and continued to in 1992; used at-large elections in 1987 and then switched to district elections; used unelected, appointed board members in 1987 and/or 1992; used ward election in 1987 and continued to in 1992; or used ward elections in 1987 and then switched to at-large elections in 1992. The reader can see these results in appendix C (see table A5.1). Here we use the information from that analysis to illustrate the importance of different selection methods by showing how black representation on the school board will vary in districts of each type with a hypothetical minority population of 10 percent African American. The results are shown in figure 5.2.

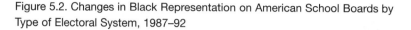

Figure 5.2. Changes in Black Representation on American School Boards by Type of Electoral System, 1987–92

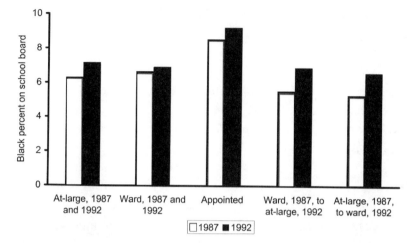

Note: The values represent the expected percentage of blacks on a school board when the school district's black residents make up 10 percent of the total population.
Source: U.S. Census of Governments, 1987 and 1992.

In figure 5.2, the gray bars represent districts in 1987 and the black bars the same districts in 1992. We see, for example, that districts that used at-large elections in 1987 and continued to use them in 1992 underrepresented African Americans; in 1987, a district of that type with a population that was 10 percent black would be expected to have slightly more than 6 percent black representation on the board. In 1992 those same districts would be likely to see slightly more than 7 percent black representation on the board, part of an overall increase we see in all types of school districts.

But overall, we find that descriptive representation is *best* achieved by avoiding elections altogether—indeed, we know from the regression analysis in appendix C that school districts in appointed systems can expect to have black representation even when there are few blacks in the community (the constant term is positive, rather than negative), and they achieve near parity on the board (8.5 percent of the school board members are expected to be black when the population is 10 per-

cent black). In contrast, there is a certain amount of underrepresentation in all types of systems using elections.

But we also see that those districts in which black representation was
most problematic in 1987—whether from at-large or district elections—were those most likely to switch in 1992. Of course, a far greater
number of districts switched from at-large to district (2,470) than from
district to at-large (405). But it is important to highlight that gains occurred from changes in *both directions*, and this suggests that voting
rights advocates and community officials themselves identified those
communities with the lowest levels of black representation (relative to
their black populations) as the ones most in need of change.

The black bars show the same districts in 1992 after many changed.
The evidence for districts that changed electoral systems is dramatic.
Though black representation improved everywhere, it improved most
markedly in those that switched to at-large elections or to ward-based
elections from what they were doing before.[14] Detailed case studies of
each district would be required to know with certainty if they changed
from court order, settlement, or the threat of litigation, but the effects
on representation of having switched are clear. In every case, the predicted district representation with a hypothetical community of 10 percent African American population increased by more than 25 percent.

In figure 5.3, we isolate those districts that changed in the wake of
the *Gingles* decision from either ward to at-large elections, or the more
common case, from at-large to ward elections. Ward to at-large changes
were, as noted above, less common than switching the other way, and
most of these changes occurred outside the South. The impact of these
changes on black representation is illustrated in the left panel of figure
5.3, which shows that the result outside the South was noticeable and
significant—an increase of nearly 40 percent in the predicted black representation with a community that is 10 percent black—but of mar-
ginal importance in the South. Districts in these states that switched to
ward-based elections actually had a slight predicted decrease in their
representation of African Americans. We restricted the analysis to
school districts that were less than 50 percent black, but that is not cru-

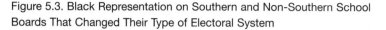

Figure 5.3. Black Representation on Southern and Non-Southern School
Boards That Changed Their Type of Electoral System

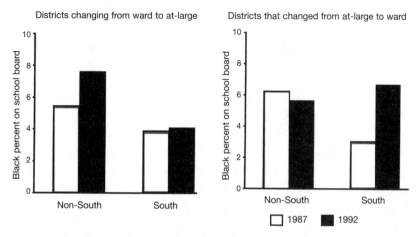

Note: The values represent the expected percentage of blacks on a school board when the
school district's black residents make up 10 percent of the total population.
Source: U.S. Census of Governments, 1987 and 1992.

cial here, because the average black population in these districts is quite
low. In a low-percentage area like these, it is unlikely that any ward would
even have a majority African American population sufficient to elect
their own candidate. Perhaps at-large elections in these areas involve
slates of candidates put together by parties or reform groups. These
slates may well be balanced by the inclusion of a minority candidate.

Within the South, the change to ward elections in over 450 districts
after *Gingles* had a dramatic impact, as depicted in the righthand panel
of figure 5.3. Whether we look at those with a minority black population (not shown) or all southern school districts considered together, we
see that many communities left untouched by the earlier quiet revolution enhanced black representation by moving to ward-based elections.
On average, the communities in this category have moderately sized
black populations of 16 percent. They show gains in representation of 121
percent between 1987 and 1992. At least in terms of descriptive representation, the effects of at-large and ward elections are as they have been
found in other studies, and our analysis of change between the time

periods offers an unprecedented look at how minority representation can be improved by changing electoral systems.

Descriptive Representation, Electoral Systems, and Policy Responsiveness

Descriptive representation is important for many reasons (Mansbridge 1999), and that is why voting rights advocates fight hard to achieve it while social scientists devote considerable computer time to understanding how electoral systems encourage or retard it. But some scholars of race (Swain 1995) and representation (Pitkin 1967) are skeptical that descriptive representation is critical, especially if it does not also promote *substantive* (or *active*) representation—policy responsiveness by another name. Under substantive representation, representatives "act for" constituencies rather than simply "standing for" them. This can be achieved through greater descriptive representation (Stewart, England, and Meier 1989), but it need not be. Is it essential for African Americans, who tend to favor high levels of spending on education, to be represented only by other African Americans?

In other words, it somewhat begs our central question to focus solely on the election of African Americans. We need to also ask whether descriptive representation fosters greater policy responsiveness. On school boards, as in other local settings, there is reason to believe that it does. In an important series of studies, Meier and his collaborators (Meier and England 1984; Meier, Steward, and England 1989) find that school boards with better African American representation are more likely to promote policies that mitigate practices that are discriminatory toward African American students. These studies are consistent with others that connect minority representation on local governments with government spending or minority government employment (Dye and Renick 1981; Mladenka 1989, 1991).

Indeed, the type of electoral system used by a community may in and of itself enhance policy responsiveness. As Lineberry and Fowler write in one of the earliest and most important studies of local government structures, "Governments which are products of the reform movement behave differently" (1967, 703). These reformed political structures "grew out of turn-of-the-century efforts to depoliticize local government" (Welch and Bledsoe 1988, 55). Their emphasis on principles of efficiency and effectiveness puts "as much distance as possible between the people and their local government" (Welch and Bledsoe 1988, 55), whereas the primacy of middle-class values of efficiency and effectiveness (Mladenka 1989) often comes at the expense of representing the views of the full community. Reformed cities govern "less on the basis of conflict and more on the basis of the rationalistic theory of administration" (Lineberry and Fowler 1967, 710), in part because these structures have both a different representational focus and representation style.[15] Residents are probably attuned to this as well, including the lack of responsiveness in reformed systems. African Americans show less sense of political efficacy in reformed than in unreformed political systems.

Reformed governments have been found to be less open and responsive to "diverse racial and socioeconomic groups" (Mladenka 1989, 175). But the racial context in which a particular system is used is important as well. Wards, Mladenka (1989) finds, may be most effective in allowing African American voices to be heard in a segregated city, whereas at-large elections may be more effective in a city that is less segregated and less defined by racial conflict. Further, different electoral systems can attract different types of minority candidates. He argues that when cities with a history of segregation use at-large systems, they are likely to attract black candidates who are unlikely to press for a redistributive agenda in order to be acceptable to the white majority.

Taken as a whole, the normative and empirical arguments can be summarized by the model of representation depicted in figure 5.4. We have seen that the type of electoral system has a powerful effect on descriptive representation in the South, with less consistent patterns in the North, and this relationship is depicted by the solid arrow in the figure. It remains to be seen whether this directly translates into greater policy responsiveness (dotted line) or whether, as suggested by Lineberry and Fowler (1967), electoral systems can affect responsive-

Figure 5.4. How Electoral Systems Can Influence Policy Responsiveness

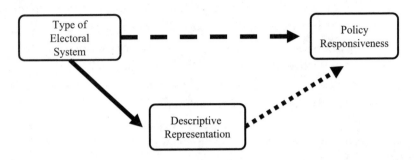

ness even without changing descriptive representation (dashed line). Of course, descriptive representation with respect to race is not an issue if no African Americans live in a particular school district, so we need to be sensitive to not only the electoral system and black electoral success but also the racial context of the community.

Policy Responsiveness in Appointed School Boards

Earlier in this chapter, we found that districts that used appointed members were more likely to have minority representation on parity with their minority populations.[16] The idea of appointing rather than electing school board officials is a Progressive one, intended to encourage the selection of people who best met ideals of administrative expertise. (Progressives valued smaller governing boards as well—see Tyack 1974—so we are not surprised to find that appointed boards tend to be smaller, with a median size of five compared with six in ward systems and seven in at-large systems). It was not the Progressives' intent to use appointments to increase black representation—Virginia, for example, adopted appointed school boards at its 1901–2 constitutional convention "explicitly because delegates feared blacks would be elected" (Morris and Bradley 1994, 286). But our findings are not completely surprising, either. Professional politicians appointing school board officials have an opportunity to balance slates racially and ethnically (Meier, Stewart, and England 1989; Taylor 2001), and black legislators in Virginia would come, later in the twentieth century, to oppose moving to school board elections because of their concern that this would make it more difficult to assure proportional black representation (Taylor 2001). It is, however, somewhat ironic that a reform intended to distance boards from their communities would come to assure them of the most proportional racial representation.

In this section, we first examine the impact of appointed school boards on policy responsiveness. In 1992, the members of 342 school boards were appointed by other elected officials. In roughly half these cases, the boards were fiscally dependent on another government, which made the appointments. This group includes all 131 Virginia school boards and 48 others scattered across six states. In addition, the members of 163 independent school districts found in fifteen states were appointed as well.

Figure 5.5. Districts with Appointed School Board Members Are More Responsive to Public Opinion Than Districts with Elected School Board Members

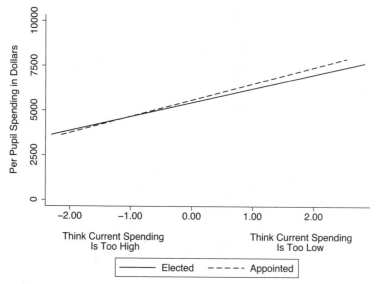

Source: Table A5.2.

Are appointed boards more or less responsive than elected ones? Figure 5.5 shows policy responsiveness (how much spending per pupil on educational expenses increases for every one unit increase in public support for spending). In this figure, the solid line represents the relationship between public opinion and spending for districts with *elected* school board members, and the dashed line represents appointed school boards (because town meetings are neither elected nor appointed, all New England towns using town meetings are excluded from this and the remaining analyses in this chapter). The line for appointed boards is significantly steeper than that for elected boards, indicating that appointed boards are about 17 percent more responsive than elected ones (see table A5.2 in appendix C for the complete regression analysis).

Work by Meier, Stewart, and England (1989) and Taylor (2001) and our analysis above show that appointed school boards better reflect the racial composition of the citizens. Could this explain why appointed school boards are more responsive than elected ones? Although it makes sense that greater descriptive representation leads to greater substantive representation, this need not be the case. Appointed boards may find themselves torn between those who appointed them and the city residents, which is largely as Progressives intended. In Virginia, for example, black members are more likely to be appointed in districts with few blacks rather than districts with many blacks (Morris and Bradley 1994, 286).

To delve into this more deeply, we need to assess whether appointed boards allow for blacks to serve on school boards where they are most needed to achieve a level of descriptive representation and then to assess policy responsiveness. We therefore divide our appointed districts into three types. First, we divide all districts into those whose population contains fewer than 5 percent African Americans and those districts with 5 percent or more. In short, we compare almost entirely white districts with those with at least a small minority presence; we call such districts *minimally diverse districts.*

The minimally diverse districts can be arrayed in terms of how closely they approach parity in descriptive representation. Perfect par-

Figure 5.6. Policy Responsiveness Is Higher in Appointed Districts but Depends on Racial Composition and Descriptive Representation

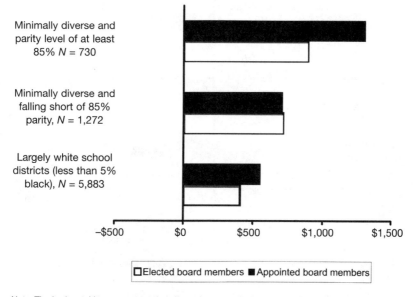

Note: The horizontal bars represent the effect of a one-unit change in public opinion on spending levels, in dollars per pupil, with all other variables at their mean.
Source: Table A5.4.

ity would mean that the percent of blacks on the school board perfectly matched that of the population. To simplify, we divide the minimally diverse districts into those that are below 85 percent of the parity level and those above 85 percent of perfect racial representation. We can now look more closely at how appointed boards foster policy responsiveness under each of these three conditions.

We then examined policy responsiveness for all three groups, and we report how the combination of racial representation and method of selection influence policy responsiveness in figure 5.6 (see table A5.4 for details). The figure shows two important trends. First, the highest levels of responsiveness occur in minimally diverse districts that have achieved high levels of African American representation on the school

Figure 5.7. In Non-Southern School Districts, Ward Elections Enhance Responsiveness in All Minimally Diverse School Districts

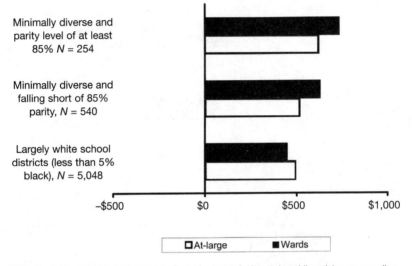

Note: The horizontal bars represent the effect of a one-unit change in public opinion on spending levels, in dollars per pupil, with all other variables at their mean.
Source: Table A5.5.

board. Second, appointed boards do not improve responsiveness in racially homogeneous school districts but do so only when there is a minimal minority presence that might otherwise lack representation *and* when the appointment method results in a level of descriptive representation that approaches parity with the population composition.

Thus, in terms of our schematic model, we find no evidence that appointment alone increases responsiveness (the dashed line in figure 5.5), but instead we find evidence that appointment increases descriptive representation which, in turn, increases responsiveness. When appointment does not lead to boards that closely mirror their community, their responsiveness is no different than elected boards.

Policy Responsiveness and Elected Boards

Clearly, appointed school boards are especially responsive. Yet they represent only a tiny fraction of all U.S. school boards. So we now move

Figure 5.8. In Southern School Districts, Neither Electoral System Nor Descriptive Representation Influences the Level of Policy Responsiveness

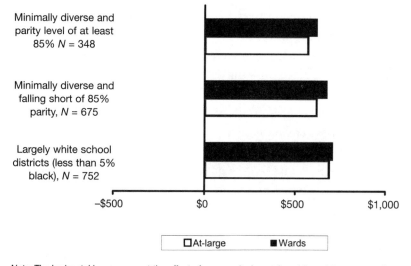

Note: The horizontal bars represent the effect of a one-unit change in public opinion on spending levels, in dollars per pupil, with all other variables at their mean.
Source: Table A5.5.

to an analysis of elected school boards. Given the history of reform and the importance of racial context, we examine the southern and non-southern states separately, by categories of racial composition and descriptive representation. We estimated our basic policy responsiveness model to see how the impact of public opinion on actual policies varies according to electoral system. The results are summarized in table A5.5 and illustrated in figure 5.7 (for non-southern districts) and figure 5.8 (southern school districts).

The results show dramatic results outside the South. In the non-southern states, policy responsiveness is enhanced by descriptive representation (compare row three with row two) and is enhanced by having a ward-based electoral system (compare the black bars with the gray ones). The exception is that wards produce slightly less responsive governance in largely white school districts, but this difference falls short of statistical significance ($t = 1.53$). Thus, in the non-southern states, both descriptive representation and electoral systems matter, and the effects are additive.

In the South, none of the six conditions have responsiveness levels that are significantly different from any other. There is a hint that wards may increase responsiveness slightly (all the black bars are slightly longer than their corresponding gray bars, and the slopes in the fourth column are a bit higher than in the third column), and there are hints that responsiveness goes down as communities become more diverse and approach parity, but these results are small and not statistically significant. In the South, the shift to ward-based elections created a quiet revolution in descriptive representation but without any corresponding gains in policy responsiveness.

Conclusion

Direct democracy is not the only way to keep local school spending in line with the preferences of the residents of America's school districts. Indirect democratic control also works. We suspected that this was the case in the previous chapter when we found, first, that town meetings are unresponsive to resident preferences and, second, that districts without direct referenda or with only limited referenda are responsive. In this chapter, we have looked in greater detail at how school board directors or members are chosen and have found that democratic control can be attained through indirect methods as well.

Policy responsiveness is only one component of democratic representation. Early in this chapter, we distinguished between passive, or descriptive, representation and active representation. Important research by Meier and his colleagues has shown that descriptive representation on American school boards is critical to active representation in certain types of school policies; for example, they have found correspondence between black representation and various school policies related to minority education. We tried to extend those findings to school spending more generally, with mixed results. But our findings on descriptive representation alone are robust, and, we believe, important for a range of policy areas beyond our blunt measure of school spending.

Descriptive representation, particularly in the South, has been enhanced by the shift to ward-based elections. School districts are not alone in recognizing that it is difficult to elect black candidates in at-large elections, at least in many settings. The Supreme Court's findings in the *Gingles* decision prodded many districts to shift to ward-based electoral systems, and the result has been an overall increase in the number of black school board members. But black representation is most assured when elections are not used at all. Appointments by other political officeholders are most easily manipulated to represent racial or ethnic minorities, and our findings show clearly that they can be used to enhance representation by African Americans. This indirect method of choosing officeholders also turns out to be the most responsive. This comes about not because school board members are appointed rather than elected but because appointments allow for racial parity.

The story for the different types of electoral systems is more complex. As with appointments, the use of wards in school districts outside the South enhances responsiveness by allowing for racial parity. Yet even without full parity in descriptive representation, we find that outside the South, wards facilitate policy responsiveness in minimally diverse school districts. One reason for this may be that officeholders elected in at-large systems have a different representational focus than those elected through wards. This is what Welch and Bledsoe (1988) find with urban governments more generally. But Mladenka (1989) has identified more complex circumstances under which wards and at-large elections allow for differences in the representation of African American interests. For example, the types of candidates chosen to run at-large—especially if they are minority in a majority white area—will differ from those selected or who self-select to run in wards. The types of coalitions these candidates build will vary as well, and Mladenka finds that the degree of segregation in the community matters as well.

Unfortunately, we cannot measure residential segregation directly, but it may help to explain the puzzling differences in policy responsiveness between the non-southern and southern states. In southern states, policy responsiveness is not contingent on either the type of electoral system used or the degree of racial representation achieved on the school board itself. But the South actually has less residential segregation than the North and Midwest (McConville et al. 2001). Though we cannot be certain, we suspect that this has something to do with our finding that the type of electoral system, and perhaps racial parity as well, are unrelated to policy responsiveness in this region.

Chapters 4 and 5 show clearly that institutions matter: Whether districts are fiscally dependent or independent, the extent to which they rely on direct democracy and the method through which officeholders are chosen all have an impact upon policy responsiveness to some degree. In the following two chapters, we change our focus somewhat away from responsiveness to public preferences to the impact of interests on school district spending. We anticipate that institutions matter here as well.

Notes

1. Susan Welch uses Joint Center for Political and Economic Studies reports to show that there were 623 black municipal officials in 1970 and 3,200 in 1987. By 2000, the Joint Center reported a total of 4,351 elected municipal officials. See http://www.jointcenter.org/DB/table/graphs/.

2. Other reforms to minimize the power of political machines included nonpartisan elections and commission or city-manager governments (Welch and Bledsoe 1988).

3. Though many associate Progressivism with political machines and northern urban governments, it actually had an enormous impact on southern and southwestern political development. At-large elections are closely associated with the commission and city-manager forms of government, and the commission originated in Galveston, Texas, from where it spread throughout the South (Davidson and Korbell 1981).

4. See Engstrom and McDonald (1981), Welch (1990), Davidson and Korbel (1981), and Meier, Stewart, and England (1989). But see MacManus (1978) for a dissenting view.

5. "Before" and "after" analyses of cities that switched electoral systems can be found in Davidson and Korbel (1981), although on cities much earlier than those covered in Welch's (1990) study.

6. The Survey of Popularly Elected Officials provides demographic information on nearly all elected, and in many cases appointed, public officials in the United States. The survey was conducted in 1967, 1977, 1987, and 1992.

7. See note 2 in chapter 4 for a list of states in each region.

8. E.g., in their study of black representation on North Carolina school boards, Arrington and Watts (1990) identify in their data those districts that required preclearance under the Voting Rights Act. Though not focusing on school districts per se, the case studies of eight southern states in Davidson and Grofman's *Quiet Revolution in the South* (1994b) give a good sense of how often southern electoral jurisdictions of all types operated under court order. As we discuss further be-

low, the 1982 amendments to the Voting Rights Act led many southern districts to abandon at-large systems.

9. This does not include other hybrids and variants, such as the "district residency require-ment" system used in North Carolina. Unfortunately, the Census of Government does not have a code for this specific type of election and codes districts inconsistently. We thank Dick Engstrom for his recommendation to code these districts as "at large."

10. *Thornburgh v. Gingles* was a North Carolina case involving multimember districts. William Brennan's majority report adopted criteria for claims of at-large vote dilution effects: First, the minority group must be large and geographically compact to constitute a majority in a single-member district, were there one; second, the group must be "politically cohesive"; and third, the majority must also vote as a bloc to "usually to defeat the minority's preferred candidate" (David-son 1994, 35).

11. E.g.: Meier and England (1984) looked at 82 large central city school districts; Robinson, England, and Meier (1985) at 168 central city school boards; Welch and Karnig (1978) at 43 cities; and Stewart, England, and Meier (1989) at 174 school districts with at least 15,000 students.

12. A less intuitive, and less widely used, measure is the subtraction method developed by MacManus (1978). For this measure, the percentage black on the governing body is subtracted from the percentage black in the community. See Welch (1990) and Engstrom and McDonald (1981) for critiques of this measure.

13. Engstrom and McDonald (1981) use a simple regression of the percentage of minority school board members on the minority percentage of the population. The regression slope, b, de-scribes the overall relationship between black population and black seats; when the slope is below 1 ($b < 1$), it means that each 1 point increase in the percentage of black residents in the commu-nity translates into less than a comparable 1 point increase in the percentage of blacks on the school board. The regression intercept also has an important substantive interpretation as the threshold for minority representation; the closer it is to 0, the more the regression coefficient can be interpreted as a direct indication of proportionality (Engstrom and McDonald 1981). When the intercept is below 0, it means there is a threshold above which blacks need a presence in the community to have any representation, whereas a positively signed intercept indicates that blacks can gain representation even when their share of the population is very low. Some researchers in-clude controls as well, for either board size or population (Bullock 1994) or black political re-sources (Stewart, England, and Meier 1989).

14. Regression analysis can be misleading when districts with black majorities are included, because under these circumstances "at-large elections should actually favor blacks" (Stewart, Eng-land, and Meier 1989, 292; see also Engstrom and McDonald 1981; Welch 1990). When we restrict the analysis to districts that have fewer than 50 percent black students, the results are not substan-tively different.

15. Welch and Bledsoe (1988) look at both *representational focus*, which is how a member de-fines the constituency, and *representational style*, which is the time spent on constituency-service functions.

16. There are more than 300 unified school boards in both fiscally dependent and fiscally in-dependent districts whose members were appointed by other elected officials. Though Stewart, England, and Meier (1989) suggest that these appointed school board members are from depen-dent school districts, the Census of Government data tell a somewhat different story. About 20 percent of dependent districts and fewer than 2 percent of independent districts used nonelected school boards (in 1987 and 1992), but nearly half of all boards with appointed officials are actu-ally fiscally independent districts.

chapter six
Teachers' Unions in State and Local Politics

 Throughout this book, we have treated public schools as political rather than market institutions. Our emphasis on responsiveness stems from a belief that school boards must be accountable and responsive to their citizens, and—unlike private schools—not focused narrowly on their consumers (Chubb and Moe 1990). But public officials are exposed to forces other than citizens' public opinion—whether this opinion is voiced through referenda or the next school board election—and in this and the following chapter we direct attention to two interests particularly critical to education politics: teachers' unions and senior citizens. Chapter 7 looks in detail at the political impact of older Americans who, we saw in chapter 3, have distinct and persistent resistance to educational spending and property taxation. Although not a formal interest group and more diverse than often recognized, the elderly do indeed act collectively in their interest.

Before we turn to the issue of what is often referred to as the "Gray Peril," we look in this chapter at the political impact of teachers' unions. Moe contends that teachers' unions "have more influence on the public schools than any other group in American society" and that unions' objectives "are often incompatible with what is best for children, schools, and society" (2001b). There are many things that teachers seek, but foremost among them are a higher salary and better benefits. In pursuing their goals, unions can have an impact on local spending levels and budgets (Hoxby 1996; Rose and Sonstelie 2004; Baugh and Stone 1982).

As we have seen with public opinion, however, political institutions mediate the ability of teachers to act collectively in pursuit of these and other goals and their influence is therefore variable across school districts. This should not surprise us. Labor unions in the United States are essentially local and state-based organizations; they were built from the bottom up. Teachers are organized at multiple levels of government, where they face different obstacles and opportunities. State laws permitting collective bargaining by public employees shape the size of local and state unions, whereas the funding regime further influences the relative effectiveness of state and local unions and the geographic distribution of education spending. We begin with an exploration of union strength throughout the United States.

American Teachers' Unions

The National Education Association (NEA) and the smaller but more urban American Federation of Teachers (AFT) have historically been and remain the most important American public school teacher unions. Both date back to the early twentieth century but emerged as formidable voices in American education during the 1960s. Traditionally, the AFT was the more militant of the two and in a critical development for the teachers' labor movement secured the right to bargain on behalf of New York City teachers in 1961 (Moe 2001b; Saltzman 1985). The NEA had traditionally been largely a professional organization, and it remains that for many of its members. But the AFT's success in New York City led the NEA, too, to fight for collective-bargaining agreements for its members. Though in the early 1960s the AFT could be fairly characterized as the only teacher union to speak of (Moe 2001b), by the late 1980s well over half the teachers in America belonged to unions.

Driving the overall trend toward greater teacher unionization was the passage of state laws that allow public employees generally and teachers specifically the right to organize and in many cases bargain collectively for district-wide contracts (Berube 1988; Lieberman 1997;

Kerchner, Koppich, and Weeres 1997). Only a handful of states had laws that defined collective-bargaining rights for public employees prior to 1955 (Farber 1988), but many more added these in the two or three decades after. The impact of these laws is thought to be cumulative over time (Hoxby 1996, 674), so by the late 1980s many states had substantial opportunity to develop teachers' unions. We see this in table 6.1, which shows the importance of state labor laws to state teachers' unions at both the state and district levels.

In table 6.1, states are grouped according to whether collective bargaining is protected and the length of time such laws have been in place: Fifteen states, nearly all in the South or Southwest, do not protect teachers' rights to bargain collectively at all. Seventeen have protected this right since before 1970, and in some cases before 1960. The remaining seventeen states have enacted these protections since 1970.[1] These state

Table 6.1. State Laws Governing Collective Bargaining and State Teachers' Unions

Type of State Laws	States	Measures of Unionization from 1987			
		No. of Unionized Teachers in the State	Percent of State's Teachers in Unions	Percent of State's Districts with Strong Unions	Percent of State's Teachers in Districts with Strong Unions
States without laws protecting collective bargaining[a]	AL, AR, AZ, CO, GA, KY, LA, MS, NC, NM, SC, TX, UT, VA, WV, WY	14,033	29.5	2.6	8.8
States with laws protecting collective bargaining since 1970	AK, CA, FL, IA, ID, IL, IN, KS, MA, MT, NH, OH, OK, PA, TN, WA	40,666	54.5	49.7	47.8
States with laws protecting collective bargaining before 1970	CT, DE, MD, ME, MI, MN, MO, ND, NE, NJ, NV, NY, OR, RI, SD, VT, WI	33,652	62.0	57.6	55.1

[a] New Mexico restored bargaining in 2003.

laws have indeed had an important and apparently cumulative impact on the development of teachers' unions. To show this, we use the most recent nationwide survey of public employee unionization, the 1987 Census of Governments. On average, fewer than one-third of teachers in the states without collective-bargaining protections are members of teachers' unions. In regions that have been historically resistant to public employee collective action—such as the South and Southwest—a few states have substantial union presence; Alabama, for example, has over 27,000 unionized teachers in the state representing over half of all teachers. But in other states, unionized teachers are a bare presence—fewer than 300 in North Carolina in the late 1980s and a mere 10 percent of all teachers in Colorado.

Even states without laws protecting collective bargaining have enough teachers with union membership—typically over 10,000—to constitute a formidable political force and organizational resource. In states with collective bargaining, upward of 50 or 60 percent of the teachers are in unions. But as Hoxby (1996) has pointed out, a simple count of unionized members does not give a full picture of their power in the state or district. Many American teachers' unions were formed "by converting existing teachers' professional associations" (Hoxby 1996, 680) and often retain more of a professional than union sensibility and mission. Their lack of militancy and identification with the larger labor movement means that their sheer numbers may well overstate their political influence.

On the basis of 1987 Census of Governments data, we construct alternate measures of union power that better account for their ability to secure benefits. The first measure codes each district as having a *strong union* (Hoxby 1996) if three conditions are met: (1) 50 percent or more of full-time teachers are members of unions, (2) the union is recognized as a collective-bargaining unit, and (3) a union contract is in place. In table 6.1, we show the proportion of districts within each state that have strong unions and the percentage of the state's teachers who are members of these strong unions as opposed to being just members of unions.

Hoxby has argued that the longer a state protects the rights of teachers to unionize, the more difficult it becomes for "a district to evade collective bargaining indefinitely" (Hoxby 1996, 683). The last two columns of table 6.1 provide compelling evidence that this is true. The difference in the number of strong districts between states without any collective-bargaining laws, those who have passed them since 1970, and those who passed them earlier is striking. Looked at in terms of union members who engage in this more complete range of collective action activities, we see that southern and southwestern states have developed few strong unions. But in states with a longer history of protecting organizing, we find that there are many districts with strong unions representing the majority of teachers.

Teachers' Unions and Policymaking Venue

Teachers have an interest in educational policy made at both the state and local levels. Policies concerning minimal standards for all schools, for example, or licensing of teachers, are made by the state, as are most initiatives to promote charter schools or vouchers. Teachers and an array of other education interests play an active role in all these, as they do in state debates on legislation affecting the very viability and health of public employee unions themselves and the fundamental design of the state funding regime. But decisions about how much teachers will receive in salary and benefits are made in two venues: the local school board and the state legislature. Teachers can influence budgeting outcomes through their activities within each venue, although their competitive environment and means of exercising influence are somewhat different in each.

In the state capital, teachers compete with other groups over the size and distribution of the state budget. In general, teacher unions will support all increases in the state education budget because public employee unions generally look to increase demand and expenditures for their services (Zax and Ichniowski 1988; Freeman 1986). In states that take on the largest share of overall funding—what we call *state-centered funding regimes*—local district budgets will be directly affected by the size of the state education budget; in state funding regimes that leave financing largely in the hands of local districts, the size of the state education budget will be less critical.

It is important to recognize that when unions are effective in increasing a state's education budget, the unions increase the flow of money to *all districts*. Though any particular union local would presumably prefer to direct limited resources to its own district, it is difficult to do this through state-level political activism. Indeed, districts without unions can benefit from union activism at the state level, allowing them in effect to ride free. This complex relationship between state-level union strength and the funding regime is summarized in the top row of table 6.2.

The most critical decisions about teachers' salaries and benefits are made by the local school district, which negotiates and approves teacher contracts. These decisions have enormous implications for final school district budgets and taxes because, as we saw in chapter 2, teacher compensation accounts for roughly half of local school districts' total operating budgets. Teacher contracts are the result of discussions among the school superintendent, the local school board, and the teachers, and there is considerable evidence showing that teachers represented by a

Table 6.2. Expected Impact of State and District Teachers' Unions on Local District Budgets

	Funding Regime	
Level	District-Centered	State-Centered
State level: As *state* unions become more powerful, there are . . .	. . . only marginal effects on district spending.	. . . higher levels of spending in all districts. Districts without strong local unions are able to free ride.
District level: As *local* unions become more powerful there are . . .	. . . *much higher* levels of spending in those districts.	. . . *somewhat* higher levels of spending in those districts.

union receive at least modestly higher salaries than teachers who are not (Kasper 1970; Hall and Carroll 1973; Baugh and Stone 1982; Eberts and Stone 1984; Easton 1988) as well as when unions are stronger rather than weaker (Hoxby 1998). Put another way, teachers are rewarded with an "experience premium" that allows for higher salaries than residents should need to pay to keep the same teachers in the district (Rose and Sonstelie 2004). This is summarized at the bottom of table 6.2: When the funding regime relies heavily on local resources, the effects of local unions' overall spending should be most pronounced. These effects will be concentrated in the districts with more powerful unions.

Unions' Political Power

As we showed above, a school district's union can be characterized as strong when the union leadership is authorized to engage in politics and collective bargaining on behalf of the membership. But the collective-bargaining status of a local union may not be sufficient to obtain a favorable contract. Teachers also want to develop a winning "political coalition" in local elections (Hoxby 1996, 676) so they can influence school board elections. Moe (2003) has argued that union *size* is therefore also a crucial source of political power; only unions with large memberships can overcome collective action problems sufficiently to influence local elections. These larger unions enjoy organizational advantages for recruiting and financing candidates, mobilizing voters (Moe 2003) and providing the labor power to form committees that will recruit, endorse, and campaign for school board candidates. Smaller unions do not have these resources, and more diffuse homeowner groups cannot "organize a union and tax themselves through union fees to support candidates aligned with their interests" (Rose and Sonstelie 2004, 2). Size therefore plays a critical role because when effective in local elections they can influence "the agenda for those facing them at the bargain table" (Freeman 1986, 42).

Therefore, when we posit in table 6.2 that more powerful unions will lead to higher per-pupil instructional expenditures we are taking a two-dimensional view of their power. On the one hand, we expect that larger unions are more formidable as political actors. On the other hand, we expect as well that unions with collective-bargaining rights will be more effective at the local level and, in general, shall be more politicized and militant in their approach to both local and state politics. Overall, we expect that teachers in strong locals are more formidable politically at both the state and local levels because they are more militant and more oriented toward using their unions for political advocacy. Therefore, we combine our indicator of collective-bargaining strength with measures of union size in order to operationalize union power at both the state and local venues.

State and Local Unions and Per-Pupil Spending

Table 6.2 shows how we expect union power at the state and local levels leads the nation's school districts to spend more or less on per-pupil instructional expenditures. In some ways, this occurs relatively directly and simply: Districts with more powerful unions, for example, should spend more than those with weaker unions. Local union strength, in other words, causes districts to spend more. But as we have seen with a good deal of the institutional analysis in this book, there are also more complex *conditional relationships*; the impact of union strength on spending, for example, should be greater when the funding regime is locally centered, placing relatively more responsibility on the district. Similarly, districts in states having strong state-level unions will tend to win higher spending at the school district level as well. But their effectiveness is proportional to the role of the state in funding local education. In the extreme case, in which the state government contributed zero to local education, even the most powerful state-level union organization could not affect local budgets. We learn from table 6.2, therefore, that we must examine the effects of union power (bargaining strength and size) both directly and as it varies systematically across the range of funding regimes.

As a first step to doing this, we show in figure 6.1 that when we properly conceive of local union power as a function of bargaining strength and size the effect on per-pupil spending is as we expected. The figure

Figure 6.1. Effect of Membership Size on Spending for Districts with and without Strong Unions

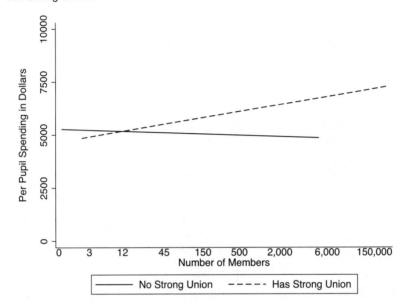

Source: Based on table A6.1, with all other variables at their mean.

is based upon analysis shown in greater detail in appendix D, and that analysis includes most of the variables we have seen in the previous few chapters (see table A6.1 in appendix D). The interpretation of figure 6.1 is no different from other interactive or conditional relationships that we have shown. In this case, the horizontal axis shows the size of the district membership logged (because of extreme values). The vertical axis shows per-pupil spending. The solid line represents districts with weak unions (see above for discussion of a weak union); the dotted line represents districts with strong unions. Clearly, the impact of union size depends on whether the union is strong or not. In nearly all cases, strong unions are associated with higher per-pupil spending. Further, the larger a strong union is at the district level, the higher we expect spending to be, holding other factors constant. Because the lines cross at a very low number of members—approximately eight to ten—we know that the negative impact of strong unions rarely occurs within the range of real school districts.[2]

We will return to the issue of local union strength below; first we explore whether strong state-level unions, too, can increase local educational spending directly through state legislative appropriations. We added to the analysis above (see table A6.2 in appendix D) the percentage of teachers in each state who are members of strong unions—a measure, we believe, of militancy at the state level. We find that stronger state unions increase per-pupil spending as well—statewide, an increase of 10 percent more teachers in strong unions leads to an additional $212 per pupil in every district in the state. There is little doubt that this is a consequence of state politics. First, close examination of the results in table A6.2 shows that the effect of local union strength persists even after accounting for the fact that strong locals are more likely than not to be in states with strong state-level organizations. And, conversely, the effectiveness of state union strength exists at least somewhat independently of local union strength. Second, when we add state educational expenditures to our model (the second model in table A6.2), we find that the importance of the state union disappears completely. This makes perfect sense: If unions increase local spending through higher state allocations, the effect of state-level union strength should disappear when we control for state expenditures that allow for higher local expenditures. The impact of state-level organizational strength is through the mechanism of increased expenditures by the state legislature.

Funding Regime and Venue

We have argued, however, that union effectiveness in maintaining high spending levels is a function of not only their power but also of the political opportunities created by the funding regime of their state. Interest groups should direct their energies at the venue where their interests are most at stake and their influence is more likely to matter. In states with very centralized funding systems, local school boards have discretion over relatively few funds and even strong local unions will have a limited impact in dollar terms. In contrast, where the state share of educational expenditures is small, strong local unions should have their greatest potential impact. This is easily tested by looking at how the relationship between both state and local union strength and per-pupil spending differs according to the nature of the state funding regime. This analysis is included in appendix D (in table A6.3), and it shows that large, strong local unions do indeed become less efficacious as the state role increases. In contrast, state-level union strength increases steadily as more and more of local budgets originate in the state capital.

To see this more clearly, we report the effects on per-pupil spending for large gains in both state and local union power under both a local-oriented funding regime and a state-centralized one. These illustrations are reported in table 6.3. Here, we can see that across the range of actual conditions, the impact of local membership declines as states play a more prominent role. This decline is sharp and is not compensated for by a correspondingly large increase in returns at the state level (cross-sectionally, a shift from 135 to 1,000 members is associated with an 11 percent increase in state strength). We believe this is because strong locals contribute to a strong statewide teachers' lobby, but the inability to redirect state funds only to their own districts dilutes these gains and spreads them to nonunionized as well as unionized school districts. This creates something of a free rider incentive for nonunionized districts to remain nonunionized and might explain the net negative impact of local unionization in the smallest districts.

Teachers' Unions and Policy Responsiveness

It is clear from the discussion above that we expect educational spending to be responsive to the interests of strong unions. But does this mean that policy is less responsive to public opinion? Not necessarily.

Any time public employees make contract demands that go beyond what residents are willing to pay, residents maintain an important option: They can always pick up and move to another community. They can also counter unions' political influence when given the "opportu-

Table 6.3. Illustration of How the Funding Regime Affects the Relative Efficacy of Local- and State-Level Unions

Effect	Bottom Fifth (38.5% state share)	Top Fifth (55.5% state share)
Effect of going from 135 to 1,000 local members in strong locals	522.22	290.90
Effect of 10% increase in state union strength	159.08	229.32

Notes: Calculations are based on the models reported in appendix table A6.3. Entries are expected increases in per-pupil spending (dollars).

nity to vote directly on referenda concerning tax collections" (Courant, Gramlich, and Rubinfield 1979, 806). So whether voting by their feet or at the ballot box, local residents can defend themselves against the possibility that unions will press for contract terms that are well outside residents' collective preferences.

But in the area of educational financing, teachers' preferences are not necessarily different from the median voter. As we showed in chapter 3, most public opinion polls show a majority of the public feels that local, state, and federal spending on public schools is *too low, rather than too high.* In particular, parents and homeowners may have a strong interest in higher spending on schools and may constitute a majority in many communities (Fischel 2001a; Rose and Sonstelie 2004). This point is important because unions' role in local school politics could be to reinforce support for parents rather than oppose them. Indeed, many residents prefer to spend more on schools than school boards do; that is why districts offering residents the opportunity to vote directly on school budgets through a referendum do not spend less than districts where the board is more insulated from the public, as we saw in chapter 4.[3] Unions, in this case, could help the broader public realize its preference to increase spending by helping to elect school board officials inclined to support higher spending or using their political power "to encourage local voters to support tax increases" (Rose and Sonstelie 2004, 5).

Figure 6.2. The Presence of Strong, Large Unions Has No Impact on Policy
Responsiveness

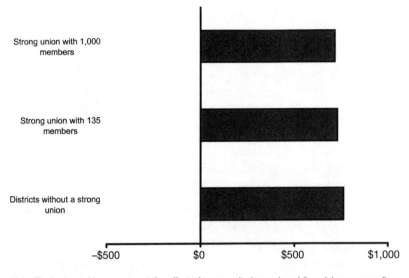

Note: The horizontal bars represent the effect of a one-unit change in public opinion on spending
levels, in dollars per pupil, with all other variables at their mean.
Source: Table A6.4.

We also expect that strong unions might have a similar impact on
responsiveness through their contract negotiations. Where referenda
rules apply, these negotiations precede the need to gain public approval.
In other districts, school board officials negotiating contracts do not
need to gain approval but must face reelection. In any referendum
game, public officeholders—in this case, the school board—go first by
proposing a policy that the public will vote on. It is at this stage that
strong unions begin to exercise their power; in effect, they set the
agenda with the school board (or their representative) through contract
negotiations. Indeed, we expect that unions are privileged over other
organized interests precisely because they can influence the budget before other groups have access to it. The result of this privileged access
is that strong unions can push for higher spending if they expect that
the public is more supportive than if the board were to expose just their

own preferences. The union knows it can push for higher spending than the board might otherwise prefer because the public will give its approval, whether through a referendum or at the next election.

We therefore explored whether responsiveness varies according to differing levels of union strength and size. Figure 6.2 shows the key results, which are based on the model in table A6.4 in appendix D. It shows that unions do not appear to either enhance or diminish responsiveness. The reason for this, we think, is that union strength is virtually uncorrelated with local opinion ($r = .08$), so union efforts to increase spending are in accord with local preferences as often as they may be in opposition—helping to increase responsiveness in thousands of districts and helping to produce somewhat higher spending than the public prefers in thousands of others. In addition, although the absolute impact of unions on spending is substantial, it is smaller than the estimated impact of local wealth and public preferences, so the signal/noise ratio of these other variables remains high.

Conclusion

In this chapter, we shifted our focus from public opinion and policy responsiveness to the influence of particular interests and American pluralism. The most important of these interests is the teachers' unions. Empowered by state laws allowing collective bargaining, teachers have established an organized presence across the American states and within American school districts. This presence, however, is uneven in size and strength; in many districts, teachers have far more power in collective bargaining and many more members to draw upon as a political resource. And in some states, collective-bargaining laws have been in place for significantly longer, giving unions more time to develop an imposing presence.

Our results confirm findings by others that these teachers' unions do increase per-pupil spending at the district level but that this influence is probably more conditional than widely recognized. The first condition is that unions need to be both *strong* and *large* to influence spending within districts. Moe (2003) and others (Hoxby 1996) have noted the political power that teachers can exert in elections, in effect choosing whom they will negotiate with. Not all unions can equally influence electoral outcomes, however; therefore, it is generally recognized that larger unions in particular will enjoy the political advantage that result from the mobilization of union resources and their ability to overcome organizational barriers.

But it is not enough for a local union to be large—it must be strong as well. Unions' strength has been emphasized by Hoxby (1996) and students of public employee unions more generally (Courant, Gramlich, and Rubinfield 1979), as has the monopoly control that unions exercise through collective bargaining. Strong unions—those with at least half a district's teachers as members, recognition as the official bargaining unit, and a bargaining agreement in place—can extract higher spending. But our analysis in this chapter also shows that *strength* and *size* interact to achieve a union's spending goals. These are the most militant unions and the ones most committed to collective action, as well as the largest, and their influence is more isolated than previously recognized.

We also find in this chapter that union influence is not restricted to the district level. On the one hand, this is not surprising. Numerous studies of state-level interest groups emphasize the strength of teachers' unions in all states. But in this chapter we show, first, that this strength is variable across states and, second, that the power of unions is shaped by the contours of the state funding regimes that determine the venue where this interest is most effective. This is a second condition on union power. Unions that are strong at the district level can aggregate their resources into statewide power. In states that take on a larger share of educational spending, union influence primarily is found at the state level, where teachers' unions compete with other organized interests over the size and distribution of state spending. These union gains find their way to all districts in the state, including those lacking strong local unions. State union strength, in other words, can undercut the power of local unions as it promotes state spending, which is distributed by formulas that do not take into account local union power.

Unions can utilize their collective-bargaining rights and their pooled resources to influence the initial selection of board members and to campaign for tax referenda and the budget proposals put up for public approval. In these varied ways, unions can successfully push for higher per-pupil spending. On average, however, this neither enhances responsiveness nor interferes with the translation of public opinion into policy. In the following chapter, we look at another important interest: the elderly. That chapter shows interesting ways in which the political impact of senior citizens is also conditional—on political institutions and on the types of seniors that are most prevalent in each community. These conditions have surprising implications for how the presence of large elderly populations affects the ability of parents and other pro-spending constituencies to realize their goals in the policy process.

Notes

1. Data on state laws were collected by F. Howard Nelson of the American Federation of Teachers. State collective bargaining laws typically include the following provisions: employee bargaining rights, scope of bargaining, unfair labor practices, dues deductions and authorization, representation and elections, a state public employee relations board and dispute resolution (e.g., fact finding, mediation, arbitration, and strikes). Of the states listed in table 6.1 as protecting collective bargaining, thirteen have laws protecting teachers specifically (as well as other public employees) and four states protect teachers only (Indiana, North Dakota, Oklahoma, and Tennessee).

2. Indeed, we noted above that districts without either strong collective bargaining or any union members at all tended to have greater resources and a greater propensity to spend so we are not surprised they can afford more spending in the absence of strong unions. But in nearly all other cases, strong union districts spend more, and the gap between strong and weak unions grows as the size of the union grows.

3. Even some teachers' workplace demands may be similar to those of parents. E.g., public employees generally may often want to increase the size of their workforce, but teachers can argue that they, like parents, simply want smaller classes. Teachers' emphasis on working conditions and equity for their members, however, could lead to a different distribution of class sizes within a district than parents would prefer.

chapter seven
The Gray Peril Reconsidered

As baby boomers age and life expectancy increases, the country's politics will be increasingly influenced by the needs and preferences of older Americans. By 2030, people over sixty-five years of age will outnumber those under twenty, reversing the nation's demographic profile (MacManus 1995). These trends are especially disturbing to education policy scholars such as Michael Kirst, who identify the growing elderly population as one of several "major societal negative forces" (Sirkin 1985) that could curtail spending on public schools. Journalistic accounts in the conventional press (e.g., Archibold 2001) and specialized venues such as the *American School Board Journal* (Wheeler 2000) and *Education Week* (e.g., Gewertz 2000; Olson 1992) echo the notion that older voters vote against school budgets, bonds, and spending increases.

In this chapter, we look at whether concentrations of older citizens constitute the "Gray Peril" (Rosenbaum and Button 1989) to school funding that many scholars, policymakers, and educators predict. Our findings in chapter 3 would appear to bear out the risk: In every public opinion survey we examined, those over sixty-five years old were less likely to support spending more on education. But there are actually no studies that directly test the Gray Peril hypothesis.[1] As we will explain, there are reasons to believe that the logic of the Gray Peril—rooted, as we will see, in the use of the property tax to fund public education—can lead many seniors to *support* spending on their neighborhood schools. We show that America's senior citizens are not a monolithic group, that public opinion polls can be misinterpreted, and that institutions can be designed in ways that minimize or exaggerate the effects of these interests.

Older Americans and Homeownership

All assertions of a looming Gray Peril rest on a combination of facts about the elderly and untested assumptions about how seniors' economic self-interest influences their politics. First, throughout the population, senior citizens are more likely to be homeowners than younger citizens (U.S. Bureau of the Census 1995). Second, homeowners on fixed incomes, such as the elderly, are especially sensitive to the property tax, the most commonly used local source for financing education, because real estate assessments increase without a similar rise in incomes. The elderly, in other words, can face progressively higher real estate tax bills without comparable increases in their income to pay for them. Third, they are of course unlikely to have children attending public school. On the basis of these facts, scholars and policymakers have assumed that elderly opposition to school spending is rooted in self-interest: They bear a substantial tax burden with no direct benefits. Because this will be true of baby boomers when they retire, it is simple to forecast a dire political context for public school finance. The logic of the Gray Peril has been very persuasive and has led many localities and states to develop tax rebates and other mechanisms to give elderly property owners, and other property owners, relief from their real estate tax bills.

Certainly, the conditions for the hypothesized Gray Peril exist throughout the United States. Seniors are more likely to own homes than all other groups throughout the nation. Yet if homeownership rates raise the prospect of a Gray Peril, political participation rates amplify the threat. At less than 20 percent of the average school district, the elderly can be influential even if they participate in local politics at the same rate as everyone else. But they do not. On four measures of local political activity, Oliver (2000) finds that older Americans participate more than younger Americans. Our own analysis of the same data used by Oliver shows that seniors are 34 percent more likely to vote in

Figure 7.1. Proportion of Homeowners Age 65 or More by School District Median Income

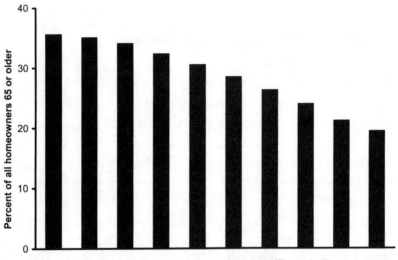

Median income from poorest to most affluent decile

Sources: Common Core of Data, National Center for Educational Statistics; U.S. Census, Special Tabulation.

local elections than those who are under forty-five—the age group most likely to have children in the public schools. This is consistent with dozens of studies of voting in national elections (e.g., Strate et al. 1989; Wolfinger and Rosenstone 1980; Rosenstone and Hansen 1993).

The elderly are disproportionately represented among homeowners and voters. But the elderly generally, and therefore older homeowners, are not equally distributed across all school districts. As we see in' figure 7.1, they are in fact much more likely to be found in poorer than wealthier districts. To create this graph, we divided all unified (K–12) American school districts into ten equal categories based on their annual median income. As we move along the horizontal axis from poorer to wealthier districts, the percentage of elderly homeowners goes down. The implications are clear: If the elderly are indeed a peril, they threaten the very districts least able to afford them.

The Gray Peril Reconsidered

The conditions underlying many people's concern with older Americans and support for public schools certainly exist. As a large and politically active group of homeowners, the elderly are likely to be affected by the impact of the property tax. They are also least likely to feel themselves directly benefiting from the tax. But we believe the Gray Peril argument is flawed. First, scholars have misinterpreted the meaning of public opinion polls; and second, they have applied an overly simplistic perspective to the role of the property tax.

As we have argued, the public opinion polls measure individuals' *general* commitment to public education. The falloff in support by older Americans has been conventionally interpreted as due to economic self-interest (e.g., Tedin, Matland, and Weiher 2001; Brokaw, Gale, and Merz 1990). However, if this argument were correct, we would see that cohorts of citizens would become increasingly conservative as they age. In fact, just the opposite occurs.

To show this, we employ the same General Social Survey data on Americans' preferences for education spending that we used in chapter 3. In table 7.1, respondents are classified according to the decade in which they were born (each row represents a different birth cohort). Representatives of each cohort were interviewed in the 1970s, 1980s, 1990s, and 2000s. If self-interest rooted in the shift to fixed incomes and the absence of school-age children were the driving forces, then as we *look across each row*, we should see steadily falling support for education spending. But the data show that *every* generation becomes increasingly *supportive* as it approaches and makes the transition into its retirement years. For example, when people born in the 1920s (the row in bold type) were interviewed in the 1970s, 50 percent said spending was too low; when representatives of this same cohort were interviewed twenty years later (when they were in their seventies), 57 percent felt that spending was too low, and this cohort was even more liberal when interviewed in their eighties. As we have shown elsewhere, the same pattern appears in the National Election Studies and in the

Table 7.1. The Percent Feeling Education Spending Is Too Low Actually Increases as Each Cohort Ages (minimum N = 50)

Decade of Respondent's Birth	Respondents Interviewed in the			
	1970s	1980s	1990s	2000s
1880s				
1890s	34	31		
1900s	40	38	53	
1910s	42	41	55	53
1920s	**50**	**47**	**57**	**64**
1930s	53	54	59	60
1940s	58	57	68	66
1950s	59	66	75	73
1960s		63	74	76
1970s			72	79
1980s			74	72

Source: General Social Survey

Illinois Policy Survey, along with consistent evidence from Harris Polls (Plutzer and Berkman 2005). On one point the evidence is overwhelming and crystal clear: People do not become more conservative toward education spending as they age—they get more liberal! The reason for this has little to do with aging per se. Rather, these are "period effects" that reflect the fact that the society as a whole has placed increasing value on public education during the past thirty years (Plutzer and Berkman 2005).

What many researchers have interpreted as a sign of self-interested, economically motivated politics is in fact a reflection of generational differences. Those born in the 1930s and 1940s grew up in a time when formal education was less important to economic security and in a day when schools claimed only a small amount of tax revenues. Thus, older Americans were socialized into a political mindset in which public schooling was just one of many important domestic priorities. Those born in later decades consistently value education near the top of their domestic agendas. But even those born many decades ago have become increasingly supportive of school spending.

At any given time, older Americans are less likely to support spending on schools, but they did not adopt these views as they aged; rather, they were always like this. The question then becomes whether older generations that have a more conservative general outlook apply that outlook to policies affecting their local schools. We suggest that there are two reasons why they may not always do so: an economic interest in maintaining high property values, and affective ties to their community's public schools.

The economic argument is fairly straightforward. Poterba (1998) makes a strong case that property value optimization may lead the elderly to actually want *higher* school expenditures; because property values are tied to school quality, it will be in their self-interest to support more, rather than less, spending. Some older citizens have long-term investments in their homes, which typically are their largest financial asset. If property values are closely tied to the perceived quality of local school systems, they may view tax increases as an investment in their long-term financial security. Of course, not all older homeowners may feel this way. Migrants in particular may have settled into certain communities precisely *because* school taxes were lower. In addition, because they no longer have children in the home, elderly migrants may be relatively unconcerned about the current quality of the schools. These recent arrivals may also be less likely to think about selling a home they recently purchased, whereas long-standing older residents may see a home sale in their future and see much of the value in their homes tied to the tax investments they have made to their communities over many decades.

In addition to economic ties to the schools, older residents—especially long-standing ones—may develop affective ties to their neighborhood schools. This is similar to Poterba's (1998) argument that the elderly may feel altruism toward children in the community, but more specific in that we posit an affective connection that varies according to how long someone has been in the community. As originally explicated by Hirschman (1970), loyalty is a powerful motivator of behavior that can conflict with instrumental self-interest. Given the wide support that appears in the public for their public schools despite their questionable performance (Hochschild and Scott 1998), as well as the central role that a school system plays in the life of a community, we should not expect older members of the community simply to "abandon" the schools as they age. Long-standing residents have roots in their community. They may have themselves attended the local schools and, if not, it is likely that their children or grandchildren did. They have likely been linked to the schools through sports, cultural activities, or community functions held on school grounds. In short, long-standing residents probably have many reasons to feel loyalty to their local public schools.

In reconsidering the Gray Peril, therefore, we not only question the theoretical basis of the argument but also point to important heterogeneity among older Americans. The combination of interest in preserving housing values and loyalty to local schools suggests an important contrast between older Americans who are new to their communities and those who have lived in the same area for a long period of time.[2] We explore these differences empirically below.

Long-Standing and Migrant Elderly

Distinguishing between older citizens who are long-standing residents of their school districts and those who are recent migrants is a complicated matter. As we have seen, the Census Bureau aggregates individual-level or block-level census data to the level of school districts in its "special tabulation." In addition to a number of variables we have already used, a detailed age breakdown was included in the special tabulation, and this allows us to measure the elderly percentage of a district's total population quite precisely. It is therefore a straightforward matter to see the percentage of all citizens who were sixty or older in 1990 (or sixty-five at the time our dependent variable is measured), and indeed we have already used these data to construct figure 7.1.

The census long form also includes a question that asks each individual where they lived five years earlier. By distinguishing between those who lived in a county for longer than five years and those who had moved within the last five years, we can distinguish between long-standing and migrant elderly. Unfortunately, this variable was *not* included in the special tabulation and is only available at the county level, which requires us to estimate the number of elderly migrants for each school district.[3] For 1,039 school districts that are coterminous with counties (e.g., all districts in Florida and South Carolina), this measure is identical to those we would find had the special tabulation measured senior citizen migration. But for the 3,422 districts that cross county lines, we needed to assign each district the weighted average of the overlapping counties, weighting according to geographic area. For the remaining 5,933 school districts wholly within a single county, we assigned to the school district the county rates.[4]

Within American school districts, the number of migrant elderly is actually relatively small. Those sixty years or older comprised 18.9 percent of the average school district in 1990; of these, 91 percent lived in the same county for over five years.[5] This leaves only 1.7 percent of the average district as recent, elderly migrants, although the range is fairly wide, with elderly migrants making up more than 5 percent of the populations of 186 districts. Figure 7.2 shows the percentage of long-standing and migrant elderly within school districts in four representative states. Florida and Nevada are characteristic of newer Sunbelt states with high overall migration, and the percentage of migrant elderly is greater in these two states. Of course, overall Nevada is much younger than Florida, as is Georgia. Pennsylvania is characteristic of states in the Rust Belt and other areas that attract few seniors from other areas and have fairly large long-standing elderly populations—in some states, the population is in effect emptying out, leaving only long-standing, increasingly elderly residents.

Long-Standing and Migrant Elderly: Drags on Spending?

Is it possible that even a 1 or 2 percent increase in elderly migrants could plausibly change the political balance enough to make a difference in policy? We expect it will and test this empirically in this section.

Figure 7.2. The Distribution of Long-Standing and Migrant Elderly in Four States

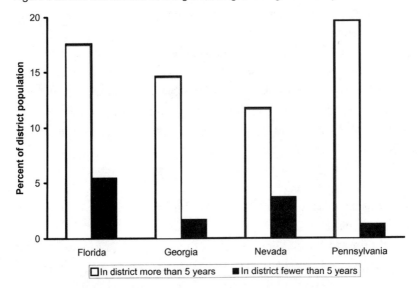

Sources: U.S. Census, Special Tabulation; Calculations from U.S. Census County-to-County Migration File.

It is important to keep in mind that our five-year definition of "recent"—necessary because of the data available from the census—is very restrictive, and we regard this as an *indicator* of elderly migrants, not the absolute number of them. Districts with more than 2 percent elderly migrants in 1990 tended to be in growing areas of the Southeast, Southwest, and Pacific regions—areas that had high levels of elderly in-migration in the 1970s and early 1980s. Thus, though it may seem implausible that 2 or 3 percent of the public could have a measurable impact on tax and spending policy, our measure underestimates the true number of relatively new arrivals (e.g., those who educated their children elsewhere and migrated in the previous ten to fifteen years) by a factor or two or more. So for that reason alone we expect to find meaningful differences across communities with different mixes of long-standing and migrant elderly.

We see in figure 7.3 that the impact of recent and long-standing el-

Figure 7.3. High Concentrations of Long-Standing Senior Citizens Increase
Educational Spending, but High Concentrations of Newly Arrived Senior
Citizens Decrease Spending

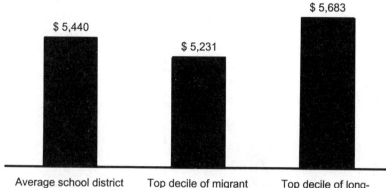

Source: Table A7.1.

derly on per-pupil spending is striking. We base this on a regression
analysis in appendix E, where it is given in table A7.1. Here we show the
effects on spending of a 5.3 percent increase in a school district of long-
standing elderly and a nearly 1 percent (0.9 percent) increase of migrant elderly. Compared with districts with average levels of seniors citizens, those at the 90th percentile in long-standing seniors spend $245
more per pupil. In contrast, those in the 90th percentile of elderly migrants spend $209 *less* for each student.

Property Tax and Circuit Breaker

If the elderly migration effect reflects sensitivity to the property tax,
the impact of elderly migrants should be greatest in places most reliant
on property taxes. In districts that receive substantial revenue from sales
or income taxes, the elderly face less of a trade-off. In economic terms,
lower reliance on the property tax lowers the *tax price* of educational
expenditures for those citizens who pay relatively more property tax
than income tax. For the long-standing elderly, the property tax may

Figure 7.4. The Effect of Property Tax Reliance on Per-Pupil Spending for Districts with Three Concentrations of Senior Citizens

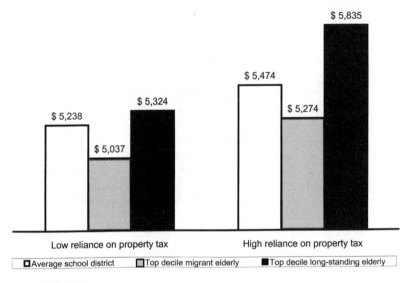

Source: Table A7.2.

play additional roles. Fischel (2001a) has argued that the more a school system depends on property taxes the better it performs, thereby protecting and enhancing home values, and presumably it enjoys greater support among voters. According to this logic, the longer that citizens have lived in their home and the greater the appreciation in value since purchase, the greater their stake in maintaining the reputation of the school system.

Indeed, closer analysis of the relationship between the elderly population in the district and per-pupil expenditures shows exactly this. We include in appendix E a regression model that allows us to assess the effect of migrant and long-standing elderly on per-pupil spending under a variety of local taxing situations (table A7.2 in appendix E). For example, we can tell through this analysis whether the effect for each group of elderly voters that we identified in figure 7.3 is the same when a school district receives relatively few revenues from the property tax or most of its funds this way. In figure 7.4, "low reliance" reflects a district receiving just 10 percent of its revenues from local property taxes, whereas "high reliance" reflects a district receiving 50 percent of its revenues from local property taxes (roughly 1 standard deviation below and above the national mean).

In figure 7.4, the impact of the long-standing elderly is seen by comparing the black bar with the white bar for any particular tax regime. We find that as reliance on the property tax increases, the positive impact of the long-standing elderly grows. If the district does not rely on property taxes at all, the impact of long-standing senior citizens is essentially zero, and it does not matter how many of them or what proportion of the district they constitute. However, if just one-third of the district's funds come from property taxes, each additional 1 percent of long-standing elderly now produces a net gain of about $46 per pupil, and their positive contribution continues to grow as districts rely more and more on property taxes. Thus, the positive impact of long-standing elderly requires the home–school linkages fostered by a funding regime that relies on property taxes. In contrast, the negative impact of elderly migrants on school spending does not depend at all on the property tax reliance. New arrivals are a drag on spending no matter the source of funds.

It seems that key premises of the gray peril hypothesis are incorrect. Large differences between seniors and others on public opinion polls are not a consequence of aging per se. In addition, for long-standing elderly migrants, sensitivity to the property tax and a low level of attitudinal support for school spending seems to be overwhelmed by a combination of loyalty and interest in maintaining high property values. New arrivals do represent something of a peril and a *real* drag on school spending—but apparently this is not due to property tax sensitivity either. This is seen in the fact that the gap between the white and gray bars is *exactly* the same for each tax regime.

These premises have rarely been seriously questioned (however, see Chew 1992). As a result, they have had important policy consequences, chief among them being the efforts to provide property tax relief to senior homeowners in the hope that they would support tax increases if they received some kind of discount or rebate. Policymakers use the term "circuit breaker" to refer to rebates to groups deemed to have especially high tax burdens (Aaron 1973; ACIR 1995). Brokaw, Gale, and Merz (1990) show that tax rebates—even when issued by the state and via the income tax system—reduce the relative tax price of increasing school budgets. Easing the tax burden of those with fixed incomes should reduce the incentive to oppose increased spending.

There are many such programs throughout the nation, and in many cases they may have started as highly targeted but then been extended to all homesteaders (e.g., Maryland); others only have an impact on the low-income elderly. Here we examine the impact of the "pure" form of circuit breaker that follows directly from the premises of the Gray Peril hypothesis: those targeted to all seniors who own homes. These pure circuit breakers exist in Arizona, Arkansas, Idaho, Ohio, and Oklahoma.

If these work as expected, elderly migrants should become less of a drag on school spending compared with both long-standing seniors and the overall community. We test this notion in a regression model reported in table A7.3 in appendix E. The table highlights spending differences in communities with an average number of elderly and above-average numbers of both long-standing and migrant elderly under two conditions: when the state boasts a circuit breaker for older homeowners and when it does not. The key results are summarized in figure 7.5. The typical effect of elderly migrants can be seen by comparing the white and gray bars in the no-rebate condition. This shows that with high concentrations of seniors who lack roots in the community, spending drops by $208 per pupil. That gap is cut to $126 in districts that have the tax rebate (the white and gray bars are closer together). In other words, in the absence of a targeted tax rebate program, elderly migrants reduce funding substantially, but with circuit breakers this is mitigated substantially. Thus the tax rebates may induce some additional support from some seniors. But at what cost?

These rebates go to all seniors who own homes, including those who are presumably supportive of the schools and need no real inducement

Figure 7.5. The Effect of Circuit Breaker Tax Rebates on Per-Pupil Spending for Districts with Three Concentrations of Senior Citizens

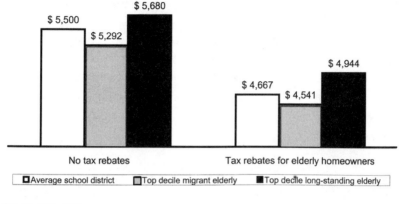

Source: Table A7.3.

to support spending increases. This represents a voluntary loss of revenue from nearly a quarter of all homeowners. The results are devastating. On average, districts in states with circuit breakers spend roughly $800 less per child. This is reflected in comparing the white and black bars in each of the three circumstances. The cleavage between long-standing elderly and senior migrants is cut by nearly half, but with an enormous drop in overall revenue for the schools.

Policy Responsiveness

Finally, we return to the question of policy responsiveness: Do large concentrations of senior citizens have a pernicious impact on the ability of the local majority to have its preferences realized in public policy? By this point in the chapter, we should be skeptical of such claims, because the presence of large numbers of seniors is associated with greater, not less, spending. To examine this more rigorously, we adopt the same approach we used in the previous chapter in our examination of unions. There we looked to see whether the relationship between opinion and per-pupil spending is either mitigated or enhanced by the presence of strong unions. Here, we look at whether the relationship between opinion and spending is affected in a substantive way by the presence of relatively large concentrations of older Americans. We find (see table A7.4 in appendix E) that the migrant elderly make no difference and that as the number of long-standing elderly increases, we see a very small—but statistically significant—*increase* in responsiveness. The regression estimates suggest that across the states, policy responsiveness would be about 8 percent lower than average if there were half as many long-standing senior citizens as there are today.

Conclusion

The Gray Peril is grossly overstated. Seniors *are* more reluctant to spend on schools than younger voters. But over time, even this group of voters has become increasingly more hospitable to spending on schools. And we find no evidence that people actually become more conservative on school spending as they age. This should reassure those who fear that the aging of America will be characterized by a reluctance to fund education. Indeed, we find just the opposite. Not only will all these aging Americans not turn against the schools, but we have strong evidence that the majority of the elderly—the long-standing elderly—actually aid the cause of citizens who support higher spending on public education.

This support by the long-standing elderly happens *only* when local school districts rely on local property taxes to generate a meaningful proportion of their total operating revenue. This once again highlights the importance of institutional design in producing specific policies and in fostering responsive governments. In this case, the evidence is very consistent with Fischel's assertion that the property tax helps to forge a close connection between the long-term financial interests of homeowners and the long-term quality and reputation of local school systems. Seniors are distinctive. But they apparently can be induced to stand alongside the interests of parents and teachers under the more traditional funding regimes. This has important implications for efforts to reform the funding regimes of American public schools—a point we discuss in greater depth in the next, concluding chapter.

None of this is meant to suggest that there is no Gray Peril at all. There is, and it manifests itself through the migration of elderly Americans to new communities where they do not have ties to the schools. For some communities, the arrival of new retirees is not only welcome but also desired and encouraged as an economic development strategy (Fagan and Longino 1993). Retirees have disposable income and appear to impose few costs: They do not increase the number of children in the schools and they commit few crimes, and the social services they do require—such as medical care—are often paid for by other levels of government. But our findings reinforce a concern McDermott (1999, 23) raises about this strategy, that over the long-term "the base will tend to diverge from the school population, which will erode willingness to pay taxes." And the measures to ameliorate such problems—for example, the use of targeted property tax circuit breaker exemptions—may well impose far higher costs on education than they save.

Notes

1. Several state-level analyses do indicate that elderly concentration is associated with lower educational spending (Poterba 1997, 1998; South 1991) but not whether school districts spend less when more elderly live in the school district. Other indirect evidence comes from studies showing that elderly voters tend to oppose tax increases when voting on school bonds and referenda (Button 1992; Muir and Schneider 1999; Lentz 1999; MacManus 1996; Tedin, Matland, and Weiher 2001; Tedin 1994), but bonds represent only a small part of the educational finance picture and do not necessarily translate into a substantial reduction in direct educational expenditures.

2. Piele and Hall (1973) suggest that recent in-migrants to a community are less likely to support the schools, whereas Lentz (1999) shows that Illinois communities with more rapid turnover and more newcomers are less likely to support education referenda. Button (1992) notes that studies of Florida have limited generalizability because the Florida elderly are often recent arrivals, many of whom are relatively wealthy, pay lower taxes than in many other states, and come initially from higher-tax northern states (Rosenbaum and Button 1989). Poterba (1997) finds evidence that states with stable elderly spend more than those with more mobile populations.

3. The census releases a massive data set detailing the characteristics of migrants for every one of the more than 9 million possible combinations of county-to-county movement. From this we were able to derive for each county the following: the total population, the number and percentage of county residents living in the county less than five years, and the number and percentage of elderly (again, sixty or over) who have lived in the county for less than five years.

4. We recognize that differences in population densities might in some cases suggest that weighting by area would give too much weight to sparsely populated counties. However, we had no clear alternative as it was impossible to disaggregate the migration data down to tracts or blocks.

5. We differentiate throughout the text between those who lived in the community or school district for more than five years, and those who migrated in within five years. Actually, we really can only determine whether residents moved into the county within five years of 1990. It is possible that some make short-distance moves, e.g., from a home to a retirement apartment complex in the same general area. Treating all these elderly as long-standing will, if anything, deflate the power of our estimates on both the long-standing and migrant elderly by mixing these migrant elderly in with long-standing elderly.

chapter eight
The Democratic Control of American School Boards

Our tour across the landscape of local American public education has taken us through time and space. American local governments were the first to take responsibility for public education, and local control remains a strong force today despite the increasing role of the states and, in more recent years, the federal government. Indeed, localism explains quite a bit about how America's public schools are organized, administered, and funded. But of equal importance is the accretion of institutional reforms such that contemporary school boards, school districts, and school-financing systems retain many characteristics they acquired in earlier times.

American federalism allows for the rich diversity in approaches to public policy and democratic governance that we find in the American public education system. We have chosen to explore this by looking broadly at thousands of school districts in forty-nine states rather than in depth at a small number of them. There is a cost in detail and color in doing this, but we believe the benefits make it well worthwhile. We have been limited to only one policy output—per-pupil instructional expenditures—but it is a critically important one that is easily comparable across districts and is directly related to almost everything schools do. Some analysts may debate whether or not increased spending leads to higher-quality education, but they cannot deny that it matters to the teachers drawing salaries and to administrators purchasing instructional materials and deciding whether to fully fund the band or art classes. Indeed, every major actor in public school politics regards educational spending as a key resource—perhaps the key resource—for achieving their educational goals.

In the 1950s and 1960s, scholars studying policy expenditures in the American states had theoretically important insights about how demographics, political institutions, and economic resources influence public policy and democratic control; the later addition of methodologically innovative measures of public opinion opened new avenues to the study of policy responsiveness as well. We believe the same level of sophistication can be brought to the study of the thousands of local governments fulfilling a myriad of critical governmental functions. We were therefore not surprised to find—but none the less gratified—that per-pupil instructional expenditures are extremely sensitive to economic, political, and demographic inputs as well as the various institutional conditions we explored throughout the analysis. Some of these inputs are well known—for example, no scholars of school finance that we know of doubt that communities with greater financial resources spend more on their schools than communities with fewer resources. But overall, our statistical models have allowed us to go beyond economic determinism and show how political choices, institutional structures, interest groups, and public opinion also shape these decisions.

The Institutional Legacy of the Progressives

We have argued that the Progressive reformers of the late nineteenth and early twentieth centuries were particularly influential in shaping the contemporary institutional landscape of American public education. But it is useful to consider a critical lesson from Stephen Skowronek's *Building a New American State* (1982): Episodes of institution building do not occur in a vacuum but rather against a backdrop of existing practices, organizations, and rules of the game. As the United States tried to build a modern administrative state, we learn in Skowronek's masterful study, it was constrained by the existing patchwork of administration by courts and political parties. Progressive efforts to rebuild American public education in one overarching model—

the "one best system"—were more successful. Nevertheless, our system still reflects the locally based, community-run schools once prevalent in much of the country, the town meetings of New England, and the political machines of urban America.

Looking across American school districts today, we find the remaining legacy of each of these, but above all we see the Progressives' handiwork. Though fragmentation into many, often small, school districts is not uncommon, especially in metropolitan areas, overall there has been substantial consolidation into larger districts. The vast majority of school districts are governed by relatively small boards of fewer than nine or even seven members, but larger and more cumbersome ones still exist. Some school districts are still part and parcel of larger and more inclusive municipal or county governments, but most are fully independent. Tax referenda are widely used to float capital bonds, but annual budgets are subject to referenda in only a limited number of states and districts. And of course, there are still those town meetings, despite the Progressives' strong dislike of them (Bryan 2004).

One Progressive innovation came up against the democratic impulses of the civil rights era. Advocates of full voting rights and equal representation recognized the pernicious effects of at-large voting systems. Responding to the Voting Rights Act and amendments to it, thousands of local governments were compelled to defend voting systems that effectively diluted the voting power of African Americans. Spurred by supporting decisions by state and federal courts, even the smallest school boards adjusted their electoral systems. Even so, as in the case of all other reforms, we find that thousands of districts of all sizes continue to use at-large voting, including more than 1,000 with substantial minority populations.

Interestingly, we have shown that at-large systems may not be discriminatory in all cases and may have advantaged African Americans in some non-southern school districts; thus it is critical that voting systems be evaluated with a sensitivity to the community's racial context. Progressives advocated appointment systems as well, perhaps not recognizing the extent to which politicians would use the opportunity to racially and otherwise balance school boards. Although it is the least widely used method of selecting school board officials, appointments are actually the most representative when measured by racial breakdown and most democratic when assessed by the standard of policy responsiveness.

State Funding Regimes

Relatively recent concerns with educational equity focused not on electoral systems or governing institutions but instead on the way state governments pay for public education. Local control preserves the ability of better-off communities to fund their schools without concern that benefits will extend to nonresidents. Zoning allows communities to maintain at least modest control over who lives in the community, for example, through limits on the number and size of multiunit dwellings. Those who cannot afford single-family houses, therefore, are unable to enjoy the benefits of many of the nation's best school systems. But local control would come under attack in the courts and the state legislatures on the grounds that it effectively denies equal access and violates state constitutional requirements of an adequate education for all state residents. The past thirty years have seen many states move to more state-centralized ways of financing their public schools.

Yet even with increased centralization, the property tax dwarfs all other financing mechanisms. Circuit breakers and tax exemptions for property owners are used in some states and localities to reduce the tax sting for subsets of property owners. But even these very generous tax exemptions are intended as a way to preserve a system that depends on property taxation, not to fundamentally change it. State governments also use their own more flexible and elastic tax systems to raise revenues for distribution to the states' school districts. In some of these districts, as much as 80 or 90 percent of all revenues comes from the state, but the remainder is still likely to be raised from the value of community property. Thus, the property tax still dominates local politics, and the amount raised by the property tax accounts for most of the intrastate differences in school spending. Only in fiscally dependent school districts, where the revenue-raising authority rests with other units of government serving a wider variety of tasks, are we likely to see significant reliance on anything other than the property tax.

Interests and the Public in Local Education Politics

Although the trend toward consolidation has created larger districts composed of people more "unlike" one another than at previous times, populations within school districts still tend to be fairly homogenous. This homogeneity is advantageous to us in our efforts to measure preferences toward spending because the method of small polity inference is especially appropriate to gauging public opinion across locales that each have limited diversity. Preferences for higher or lower education spending follow predictable and identifiable demographic cleavages, so we find significant variance in what people want when we look across the school districts within any given state or the country as a whole.

The most important political cleavages are race, age, and homeownership. Each taken alone has implications for how communities differ in their preferences for education spending. But they have even greater import when considered within the context of governing institutions, linkage mechanisms, and funding regimes. For example, given the significant difference in opinion toward higher spending between African American and white residents, the use of at-large districts that might suppress black representation is of critical importance. We believe that is why appointing rather than electing school board officeholders is so important in black communities in particular—it allows for greater African American representation in a policy area where we know African Americans hold distinct views.

Age and homeownership are of particular importance because of the property tax. In both cases—older residents and homeowners—the effects of this tax fall hardest, but we should not overstate the financial impact. For all homeowners, including the elderly who disproportionately own homes, the tax price of education is often returned when it is time to sell, and good school systems provide community benefits while the tax is being paid. The elderly do have a unique concern because they are most likely to be on fixed incomes, and this especially does seem to have an impact on the political preferences of elderly residents new to a community. Lacking the loyalty to community schools and therefore not feeling any of the "benefits" of better schools found among more long-term residents, the newly arrived elderly are clearly a drag on spending.

The mechanisms through which a group with a particular interest in education spending can influence education policy are especially clear when we look at teachers and their role in local school politics. Because our analysis uses so many school districts, we cannot tell whether the elderly are more or less organized in some communities than others or whether they disproportionately join the antitax groups that develop in some school districts. We cannot tell whether they actively participate in community budget meetings or speak up at school board meetings. And lacking survey data from school board elections, we have no way of knowing whether higher or lower taxes motivated their votes on tax increases, budgets, or school board members. But with teachers it is much easier to see how they influence policy outcomes.

Teachers are the most important formally organized interest in school politics. Because the U.S. Census Bureau was at one time more willing and able to collect and disseminate information on the local political landscape, we have a clear indication of how many teachers were union members and the particular characteristics of local unions themselves. As we have seen, teachers' unions are stronger in some school districts than others. The extent to which a state government passed laws favorable to public employee organizations appears to have had a significant and cumulative impact on whether teachers' unions did develop throughout the state.

Unions have a substantial impact on local education spending, and we were able to develop a fairly concise picture of why. Organized locally and at the state level, teachers enjoy both political influence in electoral politics and bargaining power at the local level. Again, we find that the funding regime has an unexpected impact on education politics by directing union activity toward one of two venues. Unions are powerful and active at the state level because the funding regime directs their activity that way and they can increase overall state spending and therefore spending in all the states' districts. But where the funding regime channels activity away from the state level and toward the local districts, we find much less influence from state-level unions and more based upon the power and size of the local union.

Institutions, Funding Regimes, and Education Reform Today

State governments continue to modify, restructure, and tinker with their education systems. Studying these state and local governing and fiscal institutions is therefore important not only because systems established 100 years ago continue to animate our education politics but also because they evolve—at times abruptly—yet always within the framework of long-established ways of doing things. In our home state of Pennsylvania, for example, the legislature and governor approved in the summer of 2004 a significant change in how the state pays for local education and how school boards govern. These developments highlight the continuing relevance of our findings about the effects and importance of local and state fiscal and governing institutions.

Slots and the State Funding Regime: The Case of Pennsylvania

As a longtime supporter of legalized gambling and its promised revenues, Democratic governor Edward Rendell promoted the Pennsylvania Race Horse Development and Gaming Act (2004) to allow for slot machines at select locations around the state. The state intends to use revenues from these and future gambling operations to support public education. The Homeowner Tax Relief Act (2004) distributes these revenues. It directs the state to provide local school property tax relief so long as two conditions are met: first, state gambling revenues sufficiently materialize; and second, the local school board agrees to change both how it makes decisions to increase revenues and the source of those revenues.[1] If the local school district agrees, it will be able to use the state's gambling revenues to provide property tax relief to home-owners and, in some cases, may be able to substitute state for local funds in the education budget.

Nearly every aspect of education systems discussed in the preceding chapters comes to life in the Pennsylvania tax relief program. For example, Governor Rendell was motivated by concerns with the state's funding regime that echo arguments about equity and adequacy that have resonated throughout many state legislative and court battles during the past thirty years. Noting in his 2003 inauguration address that the state share of education funding was too low and that the citizens of Pennsylvania have therefore "been forced to pay one property tax increase after another," Rendell went on to say that "I campaigned on a promise to reduce property taxes by increasing the state share of education funding. It is a promise I intend to keep. And I pledge again that this Commonwealth will honor its moral and constitutional obligation to adequately fund public education in Pennsylvania. The quality of a child's education in Pennsylvania shall never again depend on the place where that child lives."[2] Though Pennsylvania may be somewhat unusual in tying redistribution to gambling revenues and local institutional change, the pursuit of equity has been a common one in state educational politics.

School districts across Pennsylvania will need to choose whether they will participate in the state's offer of tax relief. To receive additional state funds, a district must agree to decrease its reliance on local property taxes by shifting some of its local revenue stream to a local earned or personal income tax. In doing so, it reduces its reliance on its own tax sources generally; it will use state funds to provide residents with tax relief and have the option of spending more state money directly on education operations if it shifts enough of its revenues away from property taxes.[3]

However, not all districts will gain equally by participating in Pennsylvania's plan. As under most state funding regimes, the formula for distribution of state tax money (the Property Tax Reduction Index) is based in large part on district wealth and tax effort. Districts with a high tax effort (where taxpayers pay high taxes relative to property market value and personal income levels) or relatively low wealth will be the most likely to benefit. Districts with large numbers of renters have little to gain, because they will not receive property tax exemptions, although the city of Philadelphia is exempt from much of the act. And the tax relief proposal has particular resonance for districts with many elderly, because the shift from real estate to personal income taxes will benefit residents who own property but do not work.

This change in how districts fund schools—shifting from what the Pennsylvania Economy League, a state public policy organization, calls the "steady and reliable property tax" to a combination of state and local revenues—will have implications for both the level of funding and the politics surrounding it.[4] It is important to note, as the Economy League has, that there is nothing in the act per se that increases education spending within districts. But by increasing local reliance on state funds, these reforms are likely to shift the venue for political activity. The general pattern we have seen in this study is one where states with funding regimes that favor state over local spending spend less overall, and this is not the goal of most school boards. Further, districts that rely less on the property tax—however marginally—also tend to spend less for reasons we have discussed in earlier chapters; school boards should disconnect school funding from the property tax only with great caution. And our findings about the elderly are particularly important because they suggest that long-standing elderly—and Pennsylvania is a state with a disproportionately high percentage of long-standing elderly—may help communities to maintain higher spending rather than act as a drag on it. However, the spending boost associated with long-standing elderly was greatest in those communities that relied *the most* on property taxes. By weakening the linkage between school quality and home values, Pennsylvania risks forfeiting the goodwill and loyalty that long-standing elderly have shown to the nation's public school systems.

Adopting Tax Referendum in Pennsylvania School Districts

Many Pennsylvania school board officials and advocates of higher school spending are very concerned about a looming Gray Peril. This is especially the case with regard to the second requirement for school districts; that to receive tax relief they agree to use a district-wide referendum for all future tax increases above the rate of inflation.[5] This part of the act, called the "back-end referendum," will change the finance landscape in Pennsylvania from one of the few states that provides for no direct citizen control over either school budgets or taxes to an unusual patchwork of districts where some use referenda for tax increases and others do not.

Opponents of the referendum allude to the voting power of elderly residents in particular when they voice fears that the decision to raise taxes will rest in the hands of voters, "the majority of whom have no children in school and no other district stake in their local districts" (Elizabeth and Chute 2004). The president of the Pennsylvania Educational Policy and Leadership Center, which opposed this part of the legislation, says that "school districts are going to be in this new position of going to the public for money, a public for the most part that does not have kids enrolled in the school."

School board officials throughout Pennsylvania are highly uncertain about the impact of the referendum but nevertheless are convinced that it will hurt their ability to meet spending goals. They recognize that it will, as the Pennsylvania Economy League put it, "diminish the authority traditionally held by school directors," and at least one district hired a consultant to help it puzzle through the potential impact of using a referendum.[6] But newspaper reports are full of school board officials arguing, based in large part on anecdotes from other states with the referendum, that tax increases will be rejected and overall spending lowered.[7] A spokesman from the state school board association "warned of other states in which voters have turned down tax increases and caused the collapse of programs such as marching bands, middle school sports, and libraries" (Elizabeth and Chute 2004); as the East Penn (Allentown) school board president Ann Thompson put it, "This has draconian results for us. If we opt into this and we need a new school, it's almost impossible to raise the funds." Her colleague Charles Rohrer said of state legislators, "We ought to run them out of office" (Duck 2004).

Opponents also fear that the referendum will force school boards to strategically budget in an effort to avoid a referendum vote. We suggested that this sort of referendum game might occur in our discussion in chapter 4. For example, members of the East Penn board raised the concern that the back-end referendum will encourage school boards to raise taxes to the maximum each year to ensure they have the potential to increase taxes sufficiently the next year if needed. The Pennsylvania Economy League argued that "anecdotal evidence suggests that referenda could result in lower educational performance as school boards avoid referenda by raising the student-teacher ratio, cutting new program spending, and more."

On the other side, conservative and Republican supporters of the Pennsylvania referendum provisions hold the same belief about the tax-cutting preferences of the public when faced with school board proposed tax increases. Republican supporters in the state legislature maintained that the referendum will protect homeowners from "out of control tax increases," while state senator Robert Jubillier said in support of the provision that "controlled spending" is "exactly what the referendum is intended to do and that's exactly what it will do" (Elizabeth and Chute 2004). This belief that less will be spent if only the public is allowed greater control over the budget process is well summed up by Matthew J. Brouillette, the president of the Commonwealth Foundation, a conservative group in Pennsylvania:

> Today, when a school board sits down with unionized teachers, janitors, bus drivers, or cooks, there is a blank check lying on the bargaining table. The goal of the union is to fill in the highest amount possible—and when school boards are not required to get taxpayer approval of lucrative union demands, there is little incentive for board members to say "No" to higher taxes. Hence, it is no wonder that many school employees receive compensation packages that far surpass those available in the private sector. Voter

referendum can only help us thwart the fiscally irresponsible deals pursued by labor unions. (Brouillette 2004)

Our findings suggest that opponents of referenda have less to fear from the public than they might anticipate. But they appeared, by the start of school in Fall 2005, to have won the day in most of Pennsylvania's eligible school districts. Much to the regret and disappointment of Governor Rendell, only 111 of the state's 501 school districts agreed to adopt budget referenda as a condition for accepting slots-generated revenues. "It was," said Governor Rendell, "ill-advised to ask school boards to vote to limit their own power" (Toland 2005).

Ten Thousand Democracies

America's school boards reveal two stories, an empirical one and a political one. The empirical story shows that school districts are indeed democratic. To a degree that surprised both authors of this book, there is a high correspondence between what citizens want and what they get. What they want generally is to spend more on their schools. But the commitment to spend money varies substantially across the nation, and actual spending (within the obvious constraints imposed by economic resources) reflects this variation.

Although interest groups can raise or lower spending, their efforts do not appreciably reduce policy responsiveness overall. And, with the exception of town meetings, we find no arrangement that reduces policy responsiveness to the point where one can say that democracy is seriously impaired. Given the skepticism of even the smallest legislative bodies by public choice scholars, and the belief that interest groups can hijack low-salience referenda, the consistently high level of policy responsiveness is an important finding about the American political system. Among the many meaningful variations in policy responsiveness revealed by our study, two stand out as especially provocative. School funding decisions are most responsive to public opinion in two systems that are arguably the most "political"—those in which school funding decisions are made by the more professional politicians of the city or county government, and those in which more professional politicians appoint school board members. We also saw that school districts can achieve a high level of responsiveness even when they do not reflect the social composition of their community; but at least in the North responsiveness can be higher still when school boards reflect the racial balance of the residents.

Democratic institutions in the American political system respond as well to the pluralistic interplay of particular interests, and we find that the same is true of American school districts. We have only scratched the surface of groups active in American local and state public education. But we have looked enough to know that Pennsylvania conservatives indeed have much to fear from Pennsylvania unions—they do seek higher wages and do lead to higher spending. In this state with a rich history of labor activism, we can expect to see active influence at both the state and local venues as more and more financing shifts under the new funding regime. But the referendum may not be the panacea they hope in controlling these unions, just as empowering the elderly may not be as well. Rather, we find consistent although complex evidence that organized interests are just as likely to enhance the preferences of the public as they are to subvert them.

In coming to these conclusions, we are reminded of the concluding section of Erikson, MacKuen, and Stimson's *The Macro Polity* (2002). On the last page of their monumental effort, they write that their approach to studying policy responsiveness is "of course, an early effort. We are sure that we are wrong" (p. 448). We are equally certain that future efforts to specify the conditions that enhance policy responsiveness will be better and more precise. And yet we are hopeful that the methods we have introduced here demonstrate that it is possible to study policy responsiveness at the local level. It is no longer sufficient to simply argue on theoretical grounds that one type of governance structure is more democratic than another. It is now possible to evaluate such arguments empirically.

The political story is as old as the Republic. In Pennsylvania, as in other states, the battle over democratic control of American school boards continues. The democratic wish is, James Morone (1998) eloquently teaches us, still powerful, and the fear of giving too much power to ordinary citizens continues as well. The belief of modern conservatives is no different than those who first promoted the use of referenda to limit public debt and taxation; they believe that the public will reign in its chosen policymakers. We continue to see the conflicting desires to, on the one hand, have schools run by experts exercising good judgment and, on the other hand, to control those elites with the people's voice.

School districts are natural laboratories of governance, with more than 10,000 opportunities for would-be reformers to build a better democratic system. But to see these continuing efforts as merely the policy wonk's effort to build a better mousetrap is to miss an equally important role that school districts play. For as laboratories of democracy, school districts are an arena in which we give life to the most strongly held aspirations and values that characterize the democratic wish. Reformers introduce new electoral rules or direct democracy or defend the town meeting not simply to empower those who would bring their policy preferences to the schools. They pursue these reforms to see their deepest democratic impulses and intuitions realized in their community institutions—to see them validated by being put into practice. As long as there is a democratic wish in U.S. political culture, citizens will seek to express them in the governments that are closest to the people.

Notes

1. To provide tax relief, the state must raise a minimum of $400 million in gambling revenues.

2. The text of Governor Rendell's inaugural address can be found on his website (http://www.governor.state.pa.us/governor/).

3. School districts can use state property tax relief for education operations by agreeing to increase their earned or personal income tax beyond the additional mandated amount to receive state relief; section 321 (b), (c); section 334. This and other information on the Homeowner Tax Relief Act can be found on the website of the Pennsylvania Department of Education (http://www.pde.state.pa.us/proptax/site/default.asp).

4. See "Pennsylvania's Big Gamble: An Analysis of Property Tax Relief," on the website of Pennsylvania Economy League (http://www.issuespa.net/articles/9352/).

5. The statute does allow for a wide range of exemptions for spending that will require a referendum. E.g., a district would not need to hold a referendum for tax increases for costs to implement a school improvement plan required under No Child Left Behind, minus any state funds that the district received for this purpose (http://www.pde.state.pa.us/proptax/lib/proptax/FAQ_Act72_9-21-04.pdf).

6. The East Penn school district hired David Sallack of Public Financial Management to determine how the law will affect Allentown's schools.

7. E.g., see "Battle Looms over Voting on Tax Hikes; School Districts Oppose Referendum Plan," *Pittsburgh Post-Gazette*, February 25, 2004.

Appendix A: Analysis and Supporting Tables for Chapter 3

Description of the Comprehensive Model of Individual Opinion

In chapter 3, we refer to a comprehensive hierarchical regression model. In this model, the dependent variable is the General Social Survey (GSS) spending preference question, which is scored +1 for those who believe that current spending is too low, 0 for those who say spending is about right, and −1 for those who believe current spending is too high.[1] The effects of all variables are modeled as random effects that vary across the forty-four states included in the GSS sampling frame. As is common in the estimation of hierarchical models, each independent variable is state centered. In other words, each respondent's score is calculated as the difference between their raw score and the mean score for their state (centering or "de-meaning" does not affect the magnitudes of the regression slopes; e.g., if Scholastic Aptitude Tests were scored −300 to +300, rather than 200 to 800, the estimated impact on the freshman grade point average would be precisely the same). In this way, the mean of all independent variables is zero, and the intercept represents the average opinion in the average state (for helpful discussions of centering, see Aiken and West 1991; Bryk and Raudenbush 1992). The model estimates are reported in table A3.1. The model serves as the basis for selecting the relevant demographic factors to be utilized in our application of *small polity inference*.

Details on the Method of Small Polity Inference

In the following four subsections, we provide background on the method of small polity inference. In the first three, we explain the simulation, aggregation, and Bayesian approaches to inferring *state*-level public opinion. We then show how the three major approaches are related; and from this, the logic of small polity inference becomes readily apparent. The details of the computations are provided in subsequent sections.

Table A3.1. The Impact of Demographic Variables on Spending Preferences

Variable	B[a]	SE	t	p
Intercept	.640	.009	71.72	.00
Big central city[b]	.041	.023	1.80	.08
Smaller central city	.035	.023	1.52	.14
Suburb of big city	.013	.020	.68	.50
Suburb of small city	.009	.026	.36	.72
Other urban place	.005	.020	.26	.80
Black[b]	.084	.018	4.58	.00*
Other race	−.037	.034	−1.07	.29
Hispanic	.009	.033	.28	.78
Homeowner	−.056	.015	−3.78	.00*
Parent	.013	.012	1.07	.29
Family income ($1,000s)	.001	.000	1.78	.08
Graduated high school[b]	.077	.015	5.23	.00*
Some college	.113	.028	3.98	.00*
College degree	.093	.022	4.32	.00*
Advanced degree	.157	.026	6.08	.00*
Age 25–34[b]	.009	.021	.44	.66
Age 35–44	.011	.021	.53	.60
Age 45–54	−.065	.025	−2.62	.01*
Age 55–64	−.149	.026	−5.64	.00*
Age 65–74	−.218	.026	−8.49	.00*
Age 75 and above	−.225	.036	−6.24	.00*

Note: N = 14,839, from 1985–94 General Social Survey.

[a] Bs are hierarchical regression estimates accounting for clustering within states.

[b] Omitted categories are rural residency, white, dropped out before high school, and age 18–24.

*Significant at the .05 level.

Description of the Simulation Approach

To understand the background of small polity inference, it is useful to consider the three innovative approaches upon which we build. The first of these is the method of "simulated electorates." Weber and others (1972) provide the most concise description of the approach. They first divided the population of *each state* into 192 "voter types." Then they defined each voter type by the intersection of six demographic variables; a typical voter type might be an (1) urban, (2) white, (3) female, (4) Roman Catholic, (5) age twenty to thirty-four years, and (6) professional. In the second stage, they used survey data to predict the political orientation of this and the other 191 voter types. Finally, they aggregated these predicted preferences for each state, weighting each type by its actual proportion of the state's population. The general approach of Weber and colleagues is given by the formula:

$$SimOpinion_i = \sum_k^N \varphi_k \hat{Y}_k$$

Where

$SimOpinion_i$ is the predicted political orientation for place i

φ_k is the proportion in place i of voter type k

$\hat{Y}_k$ is the predicted political orientation for voter type k

Aggregation

The method of aggregation for studying policy responsiveness has its origins in the work of Miller and Stokes (1963). They employed national survey data originally intended to study the United States as a whole and calculated average opinion scores for a selection of congressional districts. The samples were small and unreliable, and a replication using the simulation method (Erikson 1978) actually performed better.

Erikson, Wright, and McIver (1993) obtained much larger samples by pooling multiple surveys that employed identical question wording and methodology. This produced the equivalent of one "poll" of citizens for each state, and these "polls" typically had samples of 1,000 or more, with a correspondingly small sampling error. One cost of this approach is that the aggregated individual polls could span ten or more years. This would be an acceptable cost if the attitude being studied were relatively stable but would be problematic if rapidly changing opinions (or migration) meant that a relative liberal or conservative state at the time of the first poll had become a moderate state by the time of the last poll used.

Bayesian Hierarchical Models with Poststratification

Most recently, Gelman and his colleagues (Gelman and Little 1997; Park, Gelman, and Bafumi 2004) have shown that by augmenting state-level aggregation with demographic data—and by using Bayesian estimation methods—they can obtain estimates of state-level opinion that are far more valid and reliable than those obtained by aggregation alone. The intuition behind their approach is fairly simple. A poll of 1,000 Californians allows a fairly reliable estimate of overall opinion in California. But if one can only interview 100 residents of Iowa, their average opinion might not be a very good estimate for all Iowans. However, if we know that Iowa is 2 percent black, with 15 percent of its citizens over sixty-five and 23 percent of its adults holding bachelor's degrees, we can improve on the simple estimate of opinion. Some additional improvement can be achieved by reweighting the data—a standard technique used in all political and media polls. Gelman's contribution is to apply recent advances in Bayesian statistics that can weight demographic information more heavily when the aggregate estimate is based on relatively little information (e.g., relying less on reweighting in California than in Iowa).

We cannot apply the Gelman approach to school districts because no national survey permits estimating opinions for such small geographic areas. But we can adapt aspects of this approach to achieve fairly valid and reliable estimates of local opinions at the school district level.

How the Methods Are Related

To see the relationship among the three methods described above, consider the following equations for predicting the opinions of a person who is of voter type j in place k. In the *simulation* method, each voter type j is determined by the intersection of demographic variables X, ignoring geography (see the equation below for Weber et al.).

The aggregation method calculates the mean opinion for each place. It can also be thought of as a special case of simulation in which demographics are ignored and voter types are entirely determined by geography. The estimation of opinion is a simple analysis of variance in which place is the independent variable. The equation below for Erikson and others describes this analysis in regression form, where α_k is a vector of regression weights for each place k and *PLACE* denotes a vector of dummy variables for each place (with the demographic characteristics of each original survey respondent ignored). The equation below for Park and others represents the estimation process used by Park, Gelman, and Bafumi (2004, 376). Considering the three models side by side, it is easy to see that Gelman and his colleagues have simply added the two methods together—essentially treating geographic location as one additional dimension that can be used to define voter types.

Doing so would seemingly increase the data demands substantially. Park, Gelman, and Bafumi (2004) use four demographic variables to define 64 voter types in each state but adding state of residence creates $64 \times 51 = 3,264$ types.

Using ordinary least squares (OLS), estimating each type individually, and employing (say) 100 respondents per type would create a need for more than 3 million original respondents. However, hierarchical Bayesian estimation reduces the data demands enormously. Hierarchical Bayes estimates for units with few (or no) cases draw on information from other similar units, and this allows Park, Gelman, and Bafumi to estimate the partisanship of African American residents of Wyoming, even though not a single such person exists in their original survey data. In essence, Gelman's approach begins with "shrunken" dummy variable effects for place and adjusts these with additional demographic information. As they point out, this is much like postsurvey weighting of polling data to conform with known demographic compositions of electorates, which is why they refer to their method as a form of *poststratification*. To summarize the three methods:

	First-Stage Estimation	Postestimation Aggregation
(Weber et al.)	$\hat{y}_{jk} = \sum_{j.} \beta X$	$Opinion_k = \sum_{j}^{J} \varphi_{jk} \hat{Y}_{jk}$
(Erikson et al.)	$\hat{y}_{jk} = \sum_{.k} \alpha_k PLACE$	$Opinion_k = \hat{Y}_{jk}$ (none)
(Gelman et al.)	$\hat{y}_{jk} = \sum_{j.} \beta X + \sum_{.k} \alpha_k PLACE$	$Opinion_k = \sum_{j}^{J} \varphi_{jk} \hat{Y}_{jk}$

Gelman's approach differs from traditional ones in three ways. (1) It combines demographics and geography, though by itself this might not provide much of an improvement *at the state level*, as Erikson, Wright, and McIver (1993) showed. (2) It uses hierarchical Bayesian methods to reduce error variance in estimates. This could be applied to the aggregation method without the use of demographic information. Its effect in that case would be to "shrink" very high and very low opinion estimates toward the national mean—with shrinkage substantial for small states having large residuals and shrinkage quite trivial for states having very large sample sizes. (3) Poststratification weighting is a standard polling technique to account for under- or overrepresentation of major groups in a sample and restore proportions that accord closely with census estimates. This, too, could be employed alone and might have especially beneficial effects when one works with data sets (e.g., the GSS) that are not intended to produce representative state samples.

Small Polity Inference

Our challenge is different from those facing scholars of state politics: We need to make out-of-sample estimates for spatial units that are smaller than the smallest identifiable unit in national sample surveys (no national political survey identifies the school district of each respondent). We must account for the differences between, let us say, adjacent suburbs that differ substantially in their racial or age composition. Simply knowing that both are in a particular state—or even suburbs of the same central city—provides little information on how their citizens' preferences might differ. As a result, demographic information is more crucial to us than to colleagues studying states.

In addition, the Weber and Gelman models assume that basic social cleavages are comparable across places. This may be defensible for partisanship because it is shaped by nation-defining events (e.g., the New Deal and the civil rights era) and nationwide cleavages concerning labor, environmental, and moral issues. But for many issues, including school finance, one cannot assume that the differences between whites and blacks, young and old, or college graduates and high school dropouts will be the same everywhere. We therefore treat the βs in the Gelman equation as random effects that vary from context to context. Our model then can be written in the form of a hierarchical random effects model (Bryk and Raudenbush 1992):

For every place k: $y_i = \sum \beta X + \alpha + r_i$

Where

y_i is the opinion of the ith person in place k
X is a vector of place-centered demographic variables $(X_{ik} - \bar{X}_k)$
β is a vector of regression slopes
α is the mean opinion in place k
r_i is the person-level error term

The place effects, α, and demographic effects, β, are modeled as random effects, with each having a unique deviation from the average effect across the nation. This is precisely the model reported in table 3.8 in chapter 3. By substituting values of X that correspond to citizen types, it is a matter of simple algebra to calculate the opinion of each voter type in each place. Census data for each school district provide the appropriate poststratification weights. In other words, rather than adding state effects to each nationally determined voter type, we allow "place times demographic" interactions for every demographic variable. The four basic approaches can be characterized as (using OLS or a hierarchical linear model, HLM):

Simulation (Weber et al.):   Demographics alone (OLS)
Aggregation (Erikson et al.):   Place alone (OLS)
Bayes with poststratification   Place plus demographics (HLM)
  (Gelman et al.):
Small polity inference   Place plus demographics-within-
  (Berkman and Plutzer):   place (HLM)

Mechanics of the Calculations

Small polity inference requires that we construct voter types that are *mutually exclusive and exhaustive* for the polity being estimated. Unfortunately, the number and nature of possible voter types is limited by the choices made at the time of the census's school district "special tabulation." For example, it is not possible to precisely calculate the percentage of a district that is white, thirty-five to forty-four years old, college educated, home-owning parents living in a small town in the Deep South. Moreover, the census definition of categories (e.g., the classification of educational attainment or the type of community) must precisely match the categories of the survey data. Given these limitations, and of course focusing on characteristics shown to be relevant in table A3.1, we identified four different ways to divide the public into voter types.

Therefore, we estimate opinion four different ways, each based on a different available typology. We regard these as four parallel measures of the same underlying concept and, therefore, used the average of the four parallel measures. The details of our construction follow.

For each district, we can identify mutually exhaustive categories defined by state and size of place, and by race and age. In addition, we can identify the percentages who own homes and are in each of several educational categories. Thus our aggregation procedure is:

$$District\ Opinion = W_k \sum_k^K \phi_k \hat{Y}_k + W_l \sum_l^L \phi_l \hat{Y}_l + W_m \sum_m^M \phi_m \hat{Y}_m + W_n \sum_n^N \phi_n \hat{Y}_n$$

Where
k denotes voter types defined by state, age, and race
      (44 x 7 x 3 = 924 types)

l   denotes voter types defined by state and size of place
      (44 x 4 = 176 types)
m denotes voter types defined by state and education
      (44 x 5 = 220 types)
n   denotes voter types defined by state and homeownership
      (44 x 2 = 88 types)
w denotes a weight assigned to the particular type of predictor
      (equal to 1 in every instance)

This method captures both all significant individual-level predictors and all significant interactions within a cluster type. In short, we calculate a weighted average that takes advantage of information on all relevant dimensions. One challenge is determining appropriate weights—that is, which factors have the most importance in generating aggregate opinion. We considered several possibilities: arbitrarily giving equal weights, using actual district spending as a criterion and estimating weights that will produce the closest fit with actual policy outcomes, using the individual-level analysis as a guide for determining which groups of variables are most important (e.g., weighting by relative explanatory power of each cluster, using explained variance as the weighting factor), or by internal consistency. All these produced essentially similar measures and an unweighted average seemed most parsimonious, so the weights are all set to 1. The measure of opinion is scaled as a standard score (mean of 0, standard deviation of 1) with high scores indicating a preference for more spending.

Note

1. The dependent variable is ordinal, and the use of ordinal logistic regression or ordinal probit regression would achieve the same ends but without violating key regression assumptions. However, the results are essentially the same, and the use of linear regression yields regression estimates that are easier to interpret. Thus we report the results from the linear regression model here.

Appendix B: Analysis and Supporting Tables for Chapter 4

Figure 4.1 in chapter 4 is based on an ordinary least squares regression model to see how spending levels vary by fiscal dependence. Per-pupil spending is the dependent variable, and we have a dummy variable coded 1 for fiscally dependent districts and 0 for independents ones. There is no variation in dependence within many states, so we cannot estimate this as a hierarchical model. Instead, we add dummy variables for each state to account for the variety of factors that may influence the levels of spending and levels of key independent variables across the states. The slope estimates, standard errors, t-ratios and significance of each variable, along with model fit and sample size, are reported in table A4.1 (the estimates for the forty-two state dummy variables are not reported).

We also control in this model for public opinion, as well as median income and the share of all education spending in the district that comes from local

Table A4.1. Dependent School Districts Spend More Than Independent Districts

District Characteristic	B	SE	t	p
Opinion	785.37	39.62	19.82	.00
Median income	−15.94	1.59	−10.00	.00
Median housing values	−.98	.57	−1.73	.08
Population (logged)	−150.26	10.91	−13.78	.00
Dependent district	489.94	117.00	4.19	.00
Local dependence on property tax	−10.58	1.65	−6.41	.00
Property tax dependence x				
housing values	.13	.01	15.77	.00
Local share of revenues	20.79	1.37	15.17	.00
Intercept	6456.16	106.15	60.82	.00
R^2	.74			
N	8,200			

Note: Dependent variable is per-pupil instructional spending in fiscal 1995.

Table A4.2. The Impact of Public Opinion on Spending Is Higher in Dependent Districts

District Characteristic	B	SE	t	p
Opinion	767.28	39.91	19.23	.00
Dependent district	−26.01	185.47	−.14	.89
Opinion x dependent	484.60	135.23	3.58	.00
Median income	−1.16	.57	−2.05	.04
Median housing values	−15.84	1.59	−9.95	.00
Population (logged)	−150.69	10.90	−13.83	.00
Local dependence on property tax	−10.42	1.65	−6.32	.00
Property tax dependence x housing values	.13	.01	16.04	.00
Local share of revenues	20.52	1.37	14.96	.00
Intercept	6481.66	106.31	60.97	.00
R^2	.74			
N	8,200			

Note: Dependent variable is per-pupil instructional spending in fiscal 1995.

sources. To account for a conditional effect where housing values explain school spending more in communities that have the heaviest reliance on the property tax, we compute an interaction term that multiplies school spending by property tax reliance. The negative sign result on income is somewhat puzzling and appears in many models throughout the text. The reason for this is primarily multicollinearity with median housing values ($r = 0.79$) and local share of revenues ($r = 0.62$). When income is entered alone, the slope is always positive, large, and significant.

To assess the conditional nature of policy responsiveness, we add to the model an interaction term between public opinion and fiscal dependence. Throughout the book, we show the interaction between opinion and some institutional characteristic to show how that characteristic mediates the effect of opinion. In this case, we are interested in how the effect of opinion on policy differs in independent and dependent districts as well as how the effect of opinion varies by the extent to which localities rely upon their own resources. The key result, illustrated in figure 4.2, is based on the model reported in table A4.2 (again, estimates for forty-two state dummy variables are not reported).

With the interaction term included, the "main effect" on spending between dependent and independent districts is no longer statistically significant and changes sign. The reason dependent and independent districts systematically

Table A4.3. In Dependent School Districts, Policy Responsiveness Varies Substantially According to Type of Citizen Access

Type of Citizen Access	Effect of Opinion[a]	SE	t	p	R^2
Dependent on county governments with no referenda, N = 185 in 4 states	874.54	250.38	3.49	.00	.78
Dependent on municpal governments with no referenda, N = 97 in 8 states	2,081.42	570.70	3.65	.00	.78
North Carolina districts dependent on counties with tax increase refer-endum requirements, N = 119	859.53	227.82	3.77	.00	.51
Dependent on New England town meetings, N = 145 meetings in 2 states	−89.55	544.08	−.16	.87	.22

[a] Regression slope for the effect on per-pupil spending controlling for median housing values, median income, population (logged), and local share of revenues.

spend differently does not rest on this basic institutional distinction. Rather, we now know that the reason spending is higher in dependent districts is that spending is responsive to public preferences for higher spending. The positive coefficient for the interaction term (484.60) indicates the amount of policy responsiveness attributable to fiscal dependence, or looked at another way, how much responsiveness is lost by the use of independent school districts.

Figures 4.3 and 4.4 show how policy responsiveness depends on institutional rules allowing different kinds of citizen involvement in the budgetary process. Because we know that responsiveness varies by fiscal dependence, we break our analysis down into dependent and independent districts. To further assess responsiveness in districts with different kinds of citizen involvement, we *separately* estimate our baseline regression model for districts in each type of institutional arrangement; we do this first for the four kinds of citizen access that define dependent districts and then for the five kinds that define independent districts.

Table A4.4. In Independent School Districts, Policy Responsiveness Varies Substantially According to Type of Citizen Access

Type of Citizen Access	Effect of Opinion[a]	SE	t	p	R^2
Independent school districts with no referenda, N = 2,194 in 14 states	674.04	62.44	10.79	.00	.70
Independent school districts with referenda for tax increases above a specific threshold, N = 2,950 in 12 states	1017.09	74.96	13.57	.00	.37
Independent school districts with referenda for all tax increases, N =1,569 in 8 states	710.83	63.34	11.22	.00	.66
Independent school districts with annual budget referenda, N = 761 in 4 states	446.14	190.36	2.34	.02	.48
Independent school districts using town budget meetings, N = 116 in 4 states	−578.60	600.18	−.96	.34	.72

[a] Regression slope for the effect on per-pupil spending controlling for median housing values, median income, population (logged), reliance on the property tax, interaction between property tax reliance and housing values, and local share of revenues.

Again, per-pupil spending is the dependent variable, public opinion is the independent variable of interest, and we include control variables used in previous analyses (with the exception of the interaction between property tax reliance and housing values, because a large number of dependent districts do not use the property tax at all), along with dummy variables denoting each state in the analysis. We report the results in tables A4.3 and A4.4; each row shows the regression coefficient for opinion; comparing down the rows, we can see the impact of opinion in each type of district and assess responsiveness.

Appendix C: Analysis and Supporting Tables for Chapter 5

Figure 5.2 in chapter 5 describes the degree of descriptive representation of African Americans in five types of school districts. To create this graph, we ran separate regressions for five types of school districts: those that used ward-based elections in both 1987 and 1992, those that used at-large elections in both years, those that switched from wards to at-large, and those that switched from at-large to ward, and finally those that used appointed systems in both. In each case, we regressed the percentage black in the community on the percentage black on the school board. The results are reported in table A5.1.

Table A5.1. Descriptive Representation on American School Boards, 1987 and 1992

Representation	Constant	b	Predicted % on board with 10% black population	N
Representation in 1987				
At-large in both 1987 and 1992	−0.51	0.68	6.3	5,764
Ward 1987 to at-large 1992	−0.46	0.60	5.5	405
Appointed (switch and same)	2.36	0.61	8.5	374
At-large 1987 to ward 1992	−0.48	0.57	5.3	2,470
Ward in both 1987 and 1992	−0.58	0.72	6.6	1,281
Representation in 1992				
At-large in both 1987 and 1992	−0.43	0.76	7.1	5,764
Ward 1987 to at large 1992	−0.50	0.74	6.9	405
Appointed (switch and same)	1.67	0.75	9.2	374
At-large 1987 to ward 1992	−0.19	0.68	6.6	2,470
Ward in both 1987 and 1992	−0.08	0.70	6.9	1,281

Note: The dependent variables is the percent of the school board that is African American, and the independent variable is the percent of the community that is African American.

Table A5.2. Descriptive Representation on American School Boards, 1987 and 1992, Southern and Non-Southern Districts with Less than 50 Percent Black Population

Representation	Constant	b	Predicted % on board with 10% black population	% change in pre-dicted board %, 1987–92	N
A. Non-southern school districts					
Representation in 1987					
Ward to at-large, 1987–92	−.14	.56	5.4		320
At-large to ward, 1987–92	−.21	.64	6.2		1880
Representation in 1992					
Ward to at-large, 1987–92	−.02	.76	7.6	39.8	320
At-large to ward, 1987–92	−.07	.57	5.7	−9.3	1880
B. Southern school districts					
Representation in 1987					
Ward to at-large, 1987–92	−1.32	.52	3.9		64
At-large to ward, 1987–92	−.00	.30	3.0		419
Representation in 1992					
Ward to at-large, 1987–92	.20	.39	4.1	4.7	64
At-large to ward, 1987–92	.27	.64	6.7	121.4	419

Note: The dependent variable is the percent of the school board that is African American, and the independent variable is the percent of the community that is African American.

Table A5.3. The Impact of Public Opinion on Spending Is Higher in Appointed Districts

District Characteristic	B	SE	t	p
Opinion	782.48	40.03	19.55	.00
Appointed board	144.42	64.78	2.23	.03
Opinion x appointed	132.75	55.68	2.38	.02
Median income	−15.88	1.64	−9.68	.00
Median housing values	−3.64	.66	−5.51	.00
Reliance on property tax	−15.22	1.79	−8.48	.00
Reliance x values	.16	.01	17.86	.00
Population (logged)	−139.17	11.01	−12.54	.00
Local share of revenues	23.96	1.49	16.13	.00
Intercept	6491.43	107.72	60.26	.00
R^2	.74			
N	7,885			

Note: New England districts using town meetings are excluded.

Table A5.4. The Impact of Public Opinion on Spending Is Higher in Appointed Districts but Depends on Racial Composition and Descriptive Representation

District Characteristic	B	SE	t	p
A. Largely white school districts (less than 5% black)				
Opinion	409.24	49.38	8.29	.00
Appointed board	286.73	135.70	2.11	.04
Opinion x appointed	144.29	90.93	1.59	.11
Median income	−1.00	1.84	−.55	.59
Median housing values	−7.03	.77	−9.10	.00
Reliance on property tax	−13.29	2.11	−6.30	.00
Reliance x values	.19	.01	18.16	.00
Population (logged)	−156.88	13.38	−11.73	.00
Local share of revenues	21.83	1.81	12.09	.00
Intercept	6433.33	132.61	48.51	.00
R^2	.74			
N	5883 (40 states)			
B. Minimally diverse and falling short of 85% parity				
Opinion	716.65	96.24	7.45	.00
Appointed board	147.25	122.82	1.20	.23
Opinion x appointed	−5.42	126.85	−.04	.97
Median income	−34.06	4.67	−7.30	.00
Median housing values	2.50	1.56	1.60	.11
Reliance on property tax	−17.73	4.33	−4.09	.00
Reliance x values	.15	.02	6.50	.00
Population (logged)	−132.12	25.02	−5.28	.00
Local share of revenues	23.76	3.43	6.92	.00
Intercept	6272.19	220.62	28.43	.00
R^2	.80			
N	1272 (35 states)			
C. Minimally diverse and parity level of at least 85%				
Opinion	892.95	108.90	8.20	.00
Appointed board	−312.04	132.88	−2.35	.02
Opinion x appointed	411.67	139.72	2.95	.00
Median income	−37.54	5.61	−6.69	.00
Median housing values	4.81	1.85	2.59	.01
Reliance on property tax	−13.12	4.67	−2.81	.01
Reliance x values	.08	.03	3.18	.00
Population (logged)	−149.03	27.99	−5.32	.00
Local share of revenues	24.18	3.38	7.16	.00
Intercept	6431.93	249.30	25.80	.00
R^2	.86			
N	730 (34 states)			

Table A5.5. Policy Responsiveness Depends on Electoral System, Racial Composition, and Descriptive Representation

District Characteristics	31 Non-Southern States, $N = 5,782$[a]		South, $N = 1,775$[a]	
	At-Large	Wards	At-Large	Wards
Largely white school districts (less than 5% black)	492.3	448.8	688.8	707.8
Minimally diverse and falling short of 85% parity	515.1	*628.8*	616.9	675.3
Minimally diverse and parity level of at least 85%	*619.5*	*734.5*	569.3	618.7

Note: Slopes significantly different from the largely white, at-large slope are indicated in italics.

[a] Regression slope for the interaction of electoral system and racial type with public opinion on per-pupil spending controlling for median housing values, median income, population (logged), reliance on the property tax, interaction between property tax reliance and housing values, and local share of revenues.

For example, districts that used at-large elections in 1987 (regressions in the first and fourth rows) underrepresented African Americans: From the intercepts for each of these two groups (–0.51 and –0.48), we know that there is a threshold level of minority presence within the district's population below which there are unlikely to be any black representatives; and from the slope coefficients (0.68 and 0.58), we know that African American representation on the board will lag behind the percentage of African American population in the community. We use the slope and intercept to compute the expected black representation for communities that had a black population of 10 percent; these are reported in the third column. This column is used to create figure 5.2.

Figure 5.3 was created in a similar fashion, but restricted to districts with African American populations of less than 50 percent, from computations reported in table A5.2. We look separately at expected black representation in southern and non-southern districts, isolating only those that changed electoral systems.

Figure 5.5, based on table A5.3, illustrates how appointed school boards are more responsive than elected ones. To estimate responsiveness on appointed and elected school boards, we use our basic regression model from previous chapters with per-pupil educational spending as the dependent variable (along with controls and state dummy indicators), and we add a dummy variable coded 1 if the district uses appointments and 0 if it uses elections to select its school board members. Again, we interact our institutional variable of interest—in this case, selection method—with public opinion. The interaction of public opinion and the use of appointed board members is positive and statistically significant, and it shows that appointed school boards are about 17 percent more responsive than those whose members are elected. Figure 5.5 assumes that all districts have the mean value for all other variables.

Figure 5.6 shows how appointment changes responsiveness for three types of school districts and is based on three equations reported in table A5.4. The results show that appointed boards do not improve responsiveness in racially homogeneous school districts but do so only when there is a minimal minority presence that might otherwise lack representation and when the appointment method results in a level of descriptive representation that approaches parity with the population composition.

We used a similar approach to separately examine southern districts (figure 5.7) and non-southern districts (figure 5.8). For reasons of space, we do not report all six regression models. But the summary calculations are reported in table A5.5.

Appendix D: Analysis and Supporting Tables for Chapter 6

To assess how local union strength and size affect per-pupil spending, we initially estimated an ordinary least squares (OLS) regression model with measures of both strength and size. This is the first model in table A6.1 and includes all states. All states can be included because public opinion is not included in this model but will be introduced later in the chapter. "Strong union in district" is coded "1" when the local union has collective-bargaining rights and represents a majority of the teachers. Union size is the number of union members (logged because it is highly skewed).

For many of the analyses in this chapter, we employ state-level independent variables (e.g., state government spending for education). These would be perfectly predicted by (collinear with) the set of state dummy variables employed in all our regression models in chapters 4 and 5. In order, then, to account for clustering within states, these analyses use Huber-White standard errors (also known as robust standard errors). Including opinion does not change the results, and we do show this later in the chapter.

The results show that school districts with strong local unions spend, on average, $597 (or about 12 percent) more for each child but that large union memberships seem to have no effect. However, we have argued that unions may need *both* size and collective bargaining strength to be effective. We test this in the second model in table A6.1, which includes both union power measures and the interaction of the two dimensions. By the logic of statistical interactions, we then have a measure of the membership size in districts lacking a strong union and a measure of membership size in districts with strong unions in place. Here, the results tell a very different and interesting story. When we estimate the impact of membership separately for districts with and without strong unions, we see that membership has a large impact on spending only when the union is strong. Going from the mean of 135 unionized teachers to 1,000 unionized teachers (slightly less than a standard deviation increase) increases instructional spending by about $545 per pupil. The ap-

Table A6.1. Strong Unions Must Have Large Memberships to Increase Per-Pupil Spending (N = 9,122)

District Characteristic	B	Robust SE	t	p	B	Robust SE	t	p
Strong union in district	597.29	191.98	3.11	.00	−577.3	395.4	−1.46	.15
Ln (membership), no strong union	−18.90	21.40	−.88	.38	−45.6	20.4	−2.24	.03
Ln (membership), strong union					273.4	93.9	2.91	.01
Median income	11.75	15.86	.74	.46	11.7	15.5	.75	.46
Median housing values	4.19	7.60	.55	.58	3.9	7.5	.52	.61
Reliance on property tax	−8.96	11.97	−.75	.46	−9.1	11.9	−.76	.45
Reliance x values	0.14	0.04	3.26	.00	0.1	0.0	3.23	.00
Population (logged)	−89.17	60.27	−1.48	.15	−169.0	71.1	−2.38	.02
Local share of revenues	13.36	11.11	1.20	.24	13.5	11.0	1.22	.23
Intercept	4,846.42	565.95	8.56	.00	5,625.2	676.6	8.31	.00
R^2	.32				.33			

parent negative impact of a strong union is misleading, because this is the estimated impact when the union has no members (an impossibility).

In table A6.2, we add to the model the percentage of teachers in each state who are members of strong unions—a measure, we believe, of militancy at the state level. The effects on the model are dramatic. Stronger state unions increase per-pupil spending as well—statewide, an increase of 10 percent more teachers in strong unions leads to an additional $212 per pupil in every district in the state. To confirm that state-level union strength operates via state politics, we added state educational expenditures to our model. If unions increase local spending through higher state allocations, the effect of state-level union strength should disappear when we control for state expenditures. The second model in table A6.2 shows precisely this. The effect of state-level union strength is now substantively tiny: Almost all the impact of state-level organizational strength is through the mechanism of increased expenditures by the state legislature.

Table 6.3 in chapter 6 reports summary effects of how union strength in a particular venue depends on the state's funding regime. The model from which

Table A6.2. At the State Level, Union Power Increases Local Per-Pupil Spending, Primarily by Increasing State Government Expenditures for Education (*N* = 9,122)

District Characteristic	B	p	B	p
Strong union in district	−1,051.33	.03	−909.45	.01
Ln (membership), no strong union	−8.34	.67	13.02	.39
Ln (membership), strong union	216.07	.03	161.41	.02
State % teachers in strong locals	21.19	.00	2.80	.31
Median income	0.35	.98	−15.40	.05
Median housing values	1.71	.81	−0.15	.96
Reliance on property tax	−16.89	.13	−20.44	.00
Reliance x values	0.17	.00	0.16	.00
Population (logged)	−121.34	.09	−36.62	.48
Local share of revenues	19.03	.06	21.46	.00
State-level educational expenditures			6.88	.00
Intercept	4,950.45	.00	−582.18	.44
R^2	.42		.64	

these summaries were calculated appears in table A6.3. Here we add to our previous regression model a measure of the state funding regime, and interactions of this term with both district and state-level union strength. To eliminate collinearity, we drop the main effect of state union strength. This is justified on theoretic grounds because its effect is mathematically defined as the impact of state unions when the state role is zero. Because state unions should note be able to influence *local* spending levels if the state plays no role in financing the schools, this coefficient is essentially fixed at zero on theoretical grounds.

Table A6.3 shows two key findings. First, the interaction of local union strength and the state's share of local educational revenues is negative. This shows that as states play a larger role in local school finance, the influence of local unions declines. Second, the interaction of state-level union strength is positive, showing that state-level unions increase their influence as states take on a larger role in funding the public schools. The magnitudes of these two interactions are illustrated in table 6.3.

To assess whether unions influence the degree of policy responsiveness, we utilize our measure of local preferences for higher or lower educational spending. If unions have a pernicious impact on policy responsiveness, we should see two different, though related, outcomes. First, the impact of strong, large local unions should remain even after controlling for local opinion. This would

Table A6.3. The Relative Impact of State and Local Unions Depends on the Centrality of the Funding Regime

District Characteristic	B	Robust SE	t	p
Strong union in district	−1,050.57	464.31	−2.26	.03
Ln (unionized teachers) x strong union	523.05	169.55	3.08	.00
State share of educational spending	−7.71	8.31	−.93	.36
Membership in strong local x state share	−6.80	2.84	−2.40	.02
State union strength x state share	0.41	0.13	3.26	.00
Median income	1.42	13.29	.11	.92
Median housing values	2.56	6.62	.39	.70
Reliance on property tax	−14.08	10.49	−1.34	.19
Reliance x values	0.16	0.05	3.43	.00
Population (logged)	−118.96	65.99	−1.80	.08
Local share of revenues	16.01	9.17	1.75	.09
Intercept	5,346.39	879.47	6.08	.00
R^2	.53			

indicate that, on average, unionized districts spend more than the public desires. Second, tendencies toward budget maximization are expected to produce noise, and we should therefore see that the relationship between public opinion and spending is weaker as unions gain strength—a negative interaction between strong union size and public opinion.

To be consistent with all other models of policy responsiveness in this book, we shift to fixed effects regression models that include a dummy variable for each state. Table A6.4 reports three models. The first is simply a replication of the second equation in table A6.1, but restricted to states for which we have valid measures of public opinion and with dummy variables for each state. This allows for a fair comparison as we introduce our opinion measures. The effect of large, strong local unions is about $210 (compared with $273 without the state fixed effects). The second model introduces the measure of public opinion, and we see the familiar strong, positive impact. Note, however, that the main effects of strong unions and large strong unions are roughly the same as in the previous model. Thus, the net impact of local unions is roughly the same as before, and this tells us that to the extent that school districts with

Table A6.4. Local Public Opinion Neither Explains Away Nor Interacts with Local Union Power (*N* = 8,100)

District Characteristic	B	*p*
Strong union in district	−1,024.80	.00
Ln (membership), no strong union	1.00	.86
Ln (membership), strong union	*196.58*	*.00*
Opinion	761.35	.00
Opinion x strong union members	*−6.79*	*.13*
Median income	−15.95	.00
Median housing values	−0.73	.19
Reliance on property tax	−11.39	.00
Reliance x values	0.12	.00
Population (logged)	−209.94	.00
Local share of revenues	22.17	.00
Intercept	7,032.30	.00
R^2	.74	

strong local unions spend more, this is *not* because citizens in these communities also want to spend more.

To model the impact on responsiveness more precisely, we calculate the interaction between local opinion and the size of strong local unions. If union power *interferes with* the translation of public preferences into policy, this interaction term should be negative. The results are shown in the third model in table A6.4, and we see that the interaction is indeed negative, but very small, and not close to being statistically significant.

Appendix E: Analysis and Supporting Tables for Chapter 7

As in chapter 6, our initial analysis of the elderly is based on the entire sample of unified school districts, and our measure of public opinion is not included. In addition to our usual controls, the regression model controls for the overall migration rate for the school district's county, so we do not attribute to senior migrants what is a more general impact or correlate of high in-migration rates. Because the percentage of elderly migrants is highly skewed (skewness = +3.8), we use the natural log of elderly migrants; although the substantive interpretations are basically the same, this improves the specification and fit of the model substantially; see table A7.1.

In tables A7.2 and A7.3, we add interactions between property tax reliance and our two measures of elderly population size as well as circuit breaker use (coded 1 for states that used circuit breakers).

Table A7.1. Effect of Long-Standing and Migrant Elderly on Per-Pupil Instructional Expenditures ($N = 9{,}174$)

District Characteristic	B	SE	t	p
Percent of long-standing seniors	45.80	4.58	10.00	.00
Percent of senior migrants (logged)	−498.21	36.87	−13.51	.00
Median income	18.35	2.22	8.25	.00
Median housing values	6.88	.65	10.57	.00
Reliance on property tax	−1.02	1.65	−.62	.54
Reliance x values	.10	.01	10.00	.00
Population (logged)	−85.02	12.14	−7.01	.00
Local share of revenues	5.82	1.29	4.51	.00
Total in-migration rate	−4.62	2.94	−1.57	.12
Intercept	4319.03	178.60	24.18	.00
R^2	.33			

Table A7.2. Effect of Long-Standing and Migrant Elderly Depends on Property Tax Reliance ($N = 9{,}173$)

District Characteristic	B	SE	t	p
Percent of long-standing seniors	3.43	7.00	.49	.62
Reliance on property tax	−23.42	3.20	−7.32	.00
Long-standing x reliance	1.29	.16	8.04	.00
Percent of senior migrants (logged)	−471.71	55.00	−8.58	.00
Senior migrants x reliance	−.03	1.35	−.02	.98
Median income	18.21	2.23	8.16	.00
Median housing values	6.55	.66	9.98	.00
Reliance x values	.11	.01	10.81	.00
Population (logged)	−85.32	12.09	−7.05	.00
Local share of revenues	6.31	1.29	4.90	.00
Total in-migration rate	−5.90	2.93	−2.01	.04
Intercept	5055.54	199.56	25.33	.00
R^2	.32			

Table A7.3. The Effect of Migrant Elderly Is Partially Offset by Circuit Breakers, but with Substantial Net Reductions in Overall Spending Levels ($N = 9{,}173$)

District Characteristic	B	SE	t	p
Percent of long-standing seniors	33.97	4.61	7.37	.00
Circuit breaker	−1250.41	170.88	−7.32	.00
Long-standing x circuit breaker	18.30	9.97	1.84	.07
Percent of senior migrants (logged)	−490.30	37.25	−13.16	.00
Senior migrants x circuit breaker	195.68	73.88	2.65	.01
Median income	17.75	2.15	8.24	.00
Median housing values	5.75	.63	9.10	.00
Reliance on property tax	−1.65	1.60	−1.03	.30
Reliance x values	.11	.00	11.30	.00
Population (logged)	−107.06	11.80	−9.08	.00
Local share of revenues	6.53	1.25	5.22	.00
Total in-migration rate	−9.88	2.86	−3.46	.00
Intercept	5000.33	176.30	28.36	.00
R^2	.37			

Table A7.4 shows our standard responsiveness analysis.

Table A7.4 Local Public Opinion Neither Explains Away Nor Interacts with the Concentration of Elderly Migrants, but Is Slightly Enhanced by the Presence of Long-Standing Elderly (N = 8,139)

District Characteristic	B	p
Opinion	*693.40*	*.00*
Percent of long-standing seniors	15.95	.00
Long-standing x opinion	*6.83*	*.02*
Percent of senior migrants (logged)	−121.66	.00
Senior migrants x opinion	*30.64*	*.18*
Median income	−14.75	.00
Median housing values	.33	.56
Reliance on property tax	−9.74	.00
Reliance x values	.11	.00
Population (logged)	−147.42	.00
Local share of revenues	21.17	.00
Total in-migration rate	−11.01	.00
Intercept	6328.61	.00
R^2	.74	

References

Aaron, Henry. 1973. What Do Circuit-Breaker Laws Accomplish? In *Property Tax Reform*, ed. George E. Peterson. Washington, D.C.: Urban Institute Press.

ACIR (Advisory Commission on Intergovernmental Relations). 1975. *Property Tax Circuit Breakers: Current Policy and Status*. Washington, D.C.: ACIR.

———. 1995. *State Property Tax Relief: Circuit Breaker Programs—Summary of Fiscal Federalism, 1995*, vol. 1. Washington, D.C.: ACIR.

Aiken, L. S., and S. G. West. 1991. *Multiple Regression: Testing and Interpreting Interactions*. Newbury Park, Calif.: Sage.

Arceneaux, Kevin. 2002. Direct Democracy and the Link between Public Opinion and State Abortion Policy. *State Politics and Policy Quarterly* 2, no. 4: 372–87.

Archibold, Randal C. 2001. School Budgets: Many Reasons Why Voters Say No. *New York Times*, May 21.

Arrington, Theodore S., and Thomas Gill Watts. 1990. The Election of Blacks to School Boards in North Carolina. *Western Political Quarterly* 44, no. 4: 1099–1105.

Banfield, Edward C., and James Q. Wilson. 1965. *City Politics*. Cambridge, Mass.: Harvard University Press.

Baugh, William H., and Joe A. Stone. 1982. Teachers, Unions, and Wages in the 1970s: Unionism Now Pays. *Industrial and Labor Relations Review* 35, no. 3: 368–76.

Bergstrom, Theodore C., Daniel L. Rubinfeld, and Perry Shapiro. 1982. Micro-Based Estimates of Demand Functions for Local School Expenditures. *Econometrica* 50, no. 5: 1183–1205.

Berube, Maurice R. 1988. *Teacher Politics: The Influence of Unions*. New York: Greenwood Press.

Bowen, Howard. 1943. The Interpretation of Voting in the Allocation of Economic Resources. *Quarterly Journal of Economics* 58, no. 1: 27–48.

Brace, Paul, Kellie Sims-Butler, Kevin Arceneaux, and Martin Johnson. 2002. Public Opinion in the American States: New Perspectives Using National Survey Data. *American Journal of Political Science* 46, no. 1: 173–89.

Brokaw, Alan J., James R. Gale, and Thomas E. Merz. 1990. The Effect of Tax Price on Voter Choice in Local School Referenda: Some New Evidence from Michigan. *National Tax Journal* 43, no. 1: 53–60.

Brouillette, Matthew J. 2004. Pennsylvania Needs School Board Rent Control. *Lancaster Intelligencer Journal*, June 3, http://talkback.lancasteronline.com/index.php?show-topic=10129.

Bryan, Frank M. 2004. *Real Democracy: The New England Town Meeting and How It Works*. Chicago: University of Chicago Press.

Bryk, A., and S. W. Raudenbush. 1992. *Hierarchical Linear Models for Social and Behavioral Research: Applications and Data Analysis Methods*. Newbury Park, Calif.: Sage.

Bullock, Charles S., III. 1994. Section 2 of the Voting Rights Act, Districting Formats, and the Election of African Americans. *Journal of Politics* 56, no. 4: 1098–1105.

Burtless, Gary, ed. 1996. *Does Money Matter? The Effects of School Resources on Student Achievement and Adult Success*. Washington, D.C.: Brookings Institution Press.

Button, James W. 1992. A Sign of Generational Conflict: The Impact of Florida's Aging Voters on Local School and Tax Referenda. *Social Science Quarterly* 73, no. 4: 786–97.

Cain, Bruce E., and Kenneth P. Miller. 2001. The Populist Legacy: Initiatives and the Undermining of Representative Government. In *Dangerous Democracy? The Battle over Ballot Initiatives in America*, ed. Larry J. Sabato, Bruce A. Larson, and Howard R. Ernst. Lanham, Md.: Rowman & Littlefield.

Chew, Kenneth S. Y. 1992. The Demographic Erosion of Public Support for Public Education: A Suburban Case Study. *Sociology of Education* 65, no. 4: 280–92.

Chubb, John E., and Terry M. Moe. 1990. *Politics, Markets & America's Schools*. Washington, D.C.: Brookings Institution Press.

Clotfelter, Charles T. 2004. Private Schools, Segregation, and the Southern States. *Peabody Journal of Education* 79, no. 2: 74–97.

Coles, Andrienne D. 1997. Take Note: An Apology for "Old Coots" Comment. *Education Week*, March 12. http://www.edweek.org.

Courant, Paul N., Edward M. Gramlich, and Daniel L. Rubinfield. 1979. Public Employee Market Power and the Level of Government Spending. *American Economic Review* 69, no. 5: 806–17.

Cronin, Thomas E. 1989. *Direct Democracy: The Politics of Initiative, Referendum, and Recall*. Cambridge, Mass.: Harvard University Press.

Davidson, Chandler. 1994. The Recent Evolution of Voting Rights Law Affecting Racial and Language Minorities. In *Quiet Revolution in the South: The Impact of the Voting Rights Act, 1965–1990*, ed. Chandler Davidson and Bernard Grofman. Princeton, N.J.: Princeton University Press.

Davidson, Chandler, and Bernard Grofman. 1994a. Editors' Introduction. In *Quiet Revolution in the South: The Impact of the Voting Rights Act, 1965–1990*, ed. Chandler Davidson and Bernard Grofman. Princeton, N.J.: Princeton University Press.

———. 1994b. The Voting Rights Act and the Second Reconstruction. In *Quiet Revolution in the South: The Impact of the Voting Rights Act, 1965–1990*, ed. Chandler Davidson and Bernard Grofman. Princeton, N.J.: Princeton University Press.

Davidson, Chandler, and George Korbel. 1981. At-Large Elections and Minority-Group Representation: A Re-Examination of Historical and Contemporary Evidence. *Journal of Politics* 43, no. 4: 982–1005.

Downes, Thomas A., and Mona P. Shah. 1995. The Effect of School Finance Reforms on the Level and Growth of Per Pupil Expenditures. Photocopy, Tufts University, Medford, Mass.

Duck, Stacey M. 2004. East Penn Skeptical Slots Can Help Schools: Law Offering $1 Billion in Gambling Money Has Strings Attached. Allentown, Pa., *Morning Call*, October 13.

Dye, T. R., and J. Renick. 1981. Political Power and City Jobs: Determinants of Minority Employment. *Social Science Quarterly* 62, no. 3: 475–86.

Easton, Todd. 1988. Bargaining and the Determinants of Teacher Salaries. *Industrial and Labor Relations Review* 41, no. 2: 263–78.

Eberts, Randall, and Joe Stone. 1984. *Unions and Public Schools: The Effect of Collective Bargaining on American Education.* Lexington, Mass.: Lexington Books.

Elam, Stanley M. 1995. *How America Views Its Schools: The PDK/Gallup Polls, 1969–1994.* Bloomington, Ind.: Phi Delta Kappa Educational Foundation.

Elizabeth, Jane, and Eleanor Chute. 2004. Voters Get More Control over School Tax Hikes: Bill's Referendum Provision Allows Exceptions for Special Education and Some Construction Projects. *Pittsburgh Post-Gazette*, July 6.

Engstrom, Richard L., and Michael D. McDonald. 1981. The Election of Blacks to City Councils: Clarifying the Impact of Electoral Arrangements on the Seats/Population Relationship. *American Political Science Review* 75, no. 2: 344–54.

Erikson, Robert S. 1978. Constituency Opinion and Congressional Behavior: A Reexamination of the Miller-Stokes Representation Data. *American Journal of Political Science* 22, no. 3: 511–35.

Erikson, Robert S., Michael B. MacKuen, and James A. Stimson. 2002. *The Macro Polity.* New York: Cambridge University Press.

Erikson, Robert S., Gerald C. Wright, and John P. McIver. 1993. *Statehouse Democracy: Public Opinion and Policy in the American States.* New York: Cambridge University Press.

Eule, J. 1990. Judicial-Review of Direct Democracy. *Yale Law Journal* 99, no. 7: 1503–90.

Evans, William N., Sheila E. Murray, and Robert M. Schwab. 2001. The Property Tax and Education Finance: Uneasy Compromises. In *Property Taxation and Local Government Finance*, ed. Wallace E. Oates. Cambridge, Mass.: Lincoln Institute of Land Policy.

Fagan, M., and C. F. Longino Jr. 1993. Migrating Retirees: A Source of Economic Development. *Economic Development Quarterly* 7, no. 1: 98–106.

Farber, Henry S. 1988. The Evolution of Public Sector Bargaining Laws. In *When Public Sector Workers Organize*, ed. Richard B. Freeman and Casey Ichniowski. Chicago: University of Chicago Press.

Farnham, Paul G. 1990. The Impact of Citizen Influence on Local Government. *Public Choice* 64, no. 3: 201–12.

Feldstein, Martin S. 1975. Wealth, Neutrality, and Local Choice in Public Education. *American Economic Review* 65, no. 1: 75–89.

Finkel, Stephen. 1995. *Causal Analysis with Panel Data*. Sage University Paper Series on Quantitative Applications in the Social Sciences 105. Thousand Oaks, Calif.: Sage.

Fischel, William A. 2001a. *The Homevoter Hypothesis*. Cambridge, Mass.: Harvard University Press.

———. 2001b. Municipal Corporations, Homeowners, and the Benefit View of the Property Tax. In *Property Taxation and Local Government Finance*, ed. Wallace E. Oates. Cambridge, Mass.: Lincoln Institute of Land Policy.

———. 2002. School Finance Litigation and Property Tax Revolts: How Undermining Local Control Turns Voters Away from Public Education, In *Developments in School Finance, 1999–2000*, ed. William J. Fowler. Washington, D.C.: National Center for Education Statistics.

Freeman, Richard B. 1986. Unionism Comes to the Public Sector. *Journal of Economic Literature* 24, no. 1: 41–86.

Gelman, Andrew, and Thomas C. Little. 1997. Poststratification into Many Categories Using Hierarchical Logistic Regression. *Survey Methodologist* 23 (December): 127–35.

Gerber, Elisabeth R. 1996a. Legislative Response to the Threat of Popular Initiatives. *American Journal of Political Science* 40, no. 1: 99–128.

———. 1996b. Legislatures, Initiatives, and Representation: The Effects of State Legislative Institutions on Policy. *Political Research Quarterly* 49, no. 2: 263–86.

———. 1999. *The Populist Paradox: Interest Group Influences and the Promise of Direct Legislation*. Princeton, NJ: Princeton University Press.

Gewertz, Catherine. 2000. Demographic Challenges Ahead for Schools, Study Warns. *Education Week*, April 19. http://www.edweek.org.

Gold, Steven D., David M. Smith, and Stephen B. Lawton. 1995. *Public School Finance Programs of the United States and Canada, 1993–1994*. Albany: American Education Finance Association and Nelson A. Rockefeller Institute of Government, State University of New York.

Guttman, Amy. 1987. *Democratic Education*. Princeton, N.J.: Princeton University Press (rev. paperback ed., 1999).

Hall, Douglas E., and Stephen F. Knapp. 2000. The Effect of the Official Ballot Referendum Form of Meeting on Towns and School Districts. Available at www.unh.edu/nhcpps/sb2/sb2.html.

Hall, W. Clayton, and Norman E. Carroll. 1973. The Effect of Teachers' Organizations on Salaries and Class Size. *Industrial and Labor Relations Review* 26, no. 2: 834–41.

Hanushek, Eric A. 1996. School Resources and Student Performance. In *Does Money Matter? The Effects of School Resources on Student Achievement and Adult Success*, ed. Gary Burtless. Washington, D.C.: Brookings Institution Press.

Helig, Peggy, and Robert J. Mundt. 1984. *Your Voice at City Hall: The Politics, Procedures and Policies of District Representation*. Albany: State University of New York Press.

Hertert, Linda, Carolyn A. Busch, and Allan R. Odden. 1994. School Financing Inequities among the States. *Journal of Education Finance* 19, no. 3: 231–55.

Hirschman, Albert O. 1970. *Exit, Voice, and Loyalty: Responses to Decline in Firms, Organizations, and States*. Cambridge, Mass.: Harvard University Press.

Hochschild, Jennifer L., and Bridget Scott. 1998. The Polls-Trends: Governance and Reform of Public Education in the United States. *Public Opinion Quarterly* 62, no. 1: 79–120.

Hofstadter, Richard. 1965. *The Age of Reform*. New York: Alfred A. Knopf.

Howards, Irving. 1967. Property-Tax Rate Limits: A View of Local Government. In *Property Taxation: USA*, ed. Richard W. Lindholm. Madison: University of Wisconsin Press.

Hoxby, Caroline M. 1996. How Teachers' Unions Affect Education Production. *Quarterly Journal of Economics* 111, no. 3: 671–718.

———. 1998. How Much Does School Spending Depend on Family Income? The Historical Origins of the Current School Finance Dilemma. *American Economic Association Papers and Proceedings* 88, no. 2: 309–14.

Iannaccone, Lawrence, and Frank W. Lutz. 1995. The Crucible of Democracy: The Local Arena. In *The Study of Educational Politics: The 1994 Commemorative Yearbook of the Politics of Education Association*, ed. Jay D. Scribner and Donald H. Layton. Washington, D.C.: Falmer Press.

Inman, Robert P. 1978. Optimal Fiscal Reform of Metropolitan Schools: Some Simulation Results. *American Economic Review* 68, no. 1: 107–22.

Jones, Bradford, and Barbara Norrander. 1996. The Reliability of Aggregated Public Opinion Measures. *American Journal of Political Science* 40 (February): 295–309.

Just, Anne. 1980. Urban School Board Elections: Changes in the Political Environment Between 1950 and 1980. *Education and Urban Society* 12, no. 4: 421–35.

Kasper, Hirschel. 1970. The Effects of Collective Bargaining on Public School Teachers' Salaries. *Industrial Labor Relations and Review* 24, no. 1: 57–72.

Kerchner, Charles T., Julia E. Koppich, and Joseph G. Weeres. 1997. *United Mind Workers: Unions and Teaching in the Knowledge Society*. San Francisco: Jossey-Bass.

Knight Foundation. 1999. *The Community Indicators Survey* (computer file). Princeton Survey Research Associates (producer). Odum Institute for Research in Social Science, University of North Carolina at Chapel Hill (distributor).

———. 2002. *The Community Indicators Survey* (computer file). Princeton Survey Research Associates (producer). Odum Institute for Research in Social Science, University of North Carolina at Chapel Hill (distributor).

Kozol, Jonathan. 1991. *Savage Inequalities*. New York: Crown.

Ladd, Everett C. 1995. Americans on Public Education. *The Public Perspective* 6 (October–November): 22–44.

Ladd, Helen. 1975. Local Education Expenditures, Fiscal Capacity and the Composition of the Property Tax Base. *National Tax Journal* 28, no. 2: 145–58.

Lascher, Edward L., Michael G. Hagen, and Steven A. Rochlin. 1996. Gun Behind the Door? Ballot Initiatives, State Policies, and Public Opinion. *Journal of Politics* 58, no. 3: 760–76.

Lentz, Corliss. 1999. Predicting School Referenda Outcomes: Answers from Illinois. *Journal of Education Finance* 24 (Spring): 459–79.

Lieberman, Myron. 1997. *The Teachers Unions: How the NEA and AFT Sabotage Reform and Hold Students, Parents, Teachers, and Taxpayers Hostage to Bureaucracy.* New York: Free Press.

Lineberry, Robert L., and Edmund P. Fowler. 1967. Reformism and Public Policies in American Cities. *American Political Science Review* 61, no. 3: 701–16.

MacManus, Susan A. 1978. City Council Election Procedures and Minority Representation: Are They Related? *Social Science Quarterly* 59, no. 1: 153–61.

———. 1995. Taxing and Spending Politics: A Generational Perspective. *Journal of Politics* 57, no. 3: 607–29.

———. 1996. *Young and Old: Generational Combat in the 21st Century.* Boulder, Colo.: Westview Press.

———. 1997. Selling School Taxes and Bond Issues to a Generationally Diverse Electorate: Lessons from Florida Referenda. *Government Finance Review* 13 (April): 17–22.

Magleby, David B. 1984. *Direct Legislation: Voting on Ballot Propositions in the United States.* Baltimore: Johns Hopkins University Press.

Mansbridge, Jane. 1980. *Beyond Adversary Democracy.* New York: Basic Books.

———. 1999. Should Blacks Represent Blacks and Women Represent Women? A Contingent "Yes." *Journal of Politics* 61, no. 3: 628–57.

Manza, Jeff, and Fay Lomax Cook. 2002. A Democratic Polity? Three Views of Policy Responsiveness to Public Opinion in the United States. *American Politics Research* 30, no. 6: 630–67.

Manza, Jeff, Fay Lomax Cook, and Benjamin I. Page. 2002. *Navigating Public Opinion: Polls, Policy, and the Future of American Democracy.* New York: Oxford University Press.

Matsusaka, John G. 1995. Fiscal Effects of Voter Initiative: Evidence from the Last 30 Years. *Journal of Political Economy* 103, no. 3: 587–623.

———. 2001. Problems with a Methodology Used to Evaluate the Voter Initiative. *Journal of Politics* 63, no. 4: 1250–57.

McConville, Shannon, and Paul Ong, with Douglas Houston and Jordan Rickles. 2001. *Examining Residential Segregation Patterns.* Discussion Paper. Los Angeles: Ralph and Goldy Lewis Center for Regional Policy Studies, University of California, Los Angeles.

McDermott, Kathryn A. 1999. *Controlling Public Education: Localism versus Equity.* Lawrence: University of Kansas Press.

McDonagh, Eileen L. 1992. Representative Democracy and State Building in the Progressive Era. *American Political Science Review* 86, no. 4: 938–50.

———. 1993. Constituency Influence on House Roll-Call Votes in the Progressive Era, 1913–1915. *Legislative Studies Quarterly* 18 (May): 185–210.

McDonald, Laughlin. 1992. The 1982 Amendments of Section 2 and Minority Representation. In *Controversies in Minority Voting: The Voting Rights Act in Perspective*, ed. Bernard Grofman and Chandler Davidson. Washington, D.C.: Brookings Institution Press.

McDonald, Laughlin, Michael B. Binford, and Ken Johnson. 1994. Georgia. In *Quiet Revolution in the South: The Impact of the Voting Rights Act, 1965–1990*, ed. Chandler Davidson and Bernard Grofman. Princeton, N.J.: Princeton University Press.

Megdal, Sharon Bernstein. 1983. The Determination of Local Public Expenditures and the Principal Agent Relation: A Case Study. *Public Choice* 40, no. 1: 71–87.

Meier, Kenneth J., and Robert E. England. 1984. Black Representation and Educational Policy: Are They Related? *American Political Science Review* 78, no. 2: 392–403.

Meier, Kenneth J., Joseph Stewart Jr., and Robert E. England. 1989. *Race, Class, and Education: The Politics of Second-Generation Discrimination*. Madison: University of Wisconsin Press.

Miller, Warren E., and Donald Stokes. 1963. Constituency Influence in Congress. *American Political Science Review* 57, no. 1: 45–56.

Mladenka, Kenneth R. 1989. Blacks and Hispanics in Urban Politics. *American Political Science Review* 83, no. 1: 165–91.

———. 1991. Public-Employee Unions, Reformism, and Black Employment in 1,200 American Cities. *Urban Affairs Review* 26, no. 4: 532–48.

Moe, Terry M. 2001a. *Schools, Vouchers, and the American Public*. Washington, D.C.: Brookings Institution Press.

———. 2001b. A Union by Any Other Name. Available at http://www.educationnext. org/20013/38moe.html.

———. 2003. Teacher Unions and School Board Elections. Paper prepared for School Board Politics Conference, Harvard University, Cambridge, Mass.

Moffitt, Robert, David Ribar, and Mark Wilhelm. 1998. The Decline of Welfare Benefits in the U.S.: The Role of Wage Inequality. *Journal of Public Economics* 68, no. 3: 421–52.

Morone, James A. 1998. *The Democratic Wish: Popular Participation and the Limits of American Government*. New Haven, Conn.: Yale University Press.

Morris, Thomas R., and Neil Bradley. 1994. Virginia. In *Quiet Revolution in the South: The Impact of the Voting Rights Act, 1965–1990*, ed. Chandler Davidson and Bernard Grofman. Princeton, N.J.: Princeton University Press.

Muir, Edward, and Krista Schneider. 1999. State Initiatives and Referenda on Bonds: A Comparative Analysis of One Solution for the School Infrastructure Crisis. *Journal of Education Finance* 24, no. 4: 415–33.

Murray, Sheila, William Evans, and Robert Schwab. 1998. Education Finance Reform and the Distribution of Education Resources. *American Economic Review* 88, no. 4: 789–812.

Oates, Wallace E., ed. 2001. *Property Taxation and Local Government Finance*. Cambridge, Mass.: Lincoln Institute of Land Policy.

Odden, Allan R., and Lawrence O. Picus. 2004. *School Finance: A Policy Perspective*, 3rd ed. New York: McGraw-Hill.

Oliver, J. 2000. City Size and Civic Involvement in Metropolitan America. *American Political Science Review* 94, no. 2: 361–73.

Olson, Lynn. 1992. Boards of Contention: Tales of Two Boards. *Education Week*, April 29. http://www.edweek.org.

Page, Benjamin I. 1994. Democratic Responsiveness? Untangling the Links between Public Opinion and Policy. *PS* 27, no. 1: 25–29.

Page, Benjamin I., and Robert Y. Shapiro. 1992. *The Rational Public: Fifty Years of Trends in Americans' Policy Preferences*. Chicago: University of Chicago Press.

Park, David K., Andrew Gelman, and Joseph Bafumi. 2004. Bayesian Multilevel Estimation with Poststratification: State-Level Estimates from National Polls. *Political Analysis* 12 (fall): 375–85.

Peterson, Paul E. 1995. *The Price of Federalism*. Washington, D.C.: Brookings Institution Press.

Piele, Philip, and John Stuart Hall. 1973. *Budget, Bonds, and Ballots: Voting Behavior in School Financial Elections*. Lexington, Mass.: Lexington Books.

Pitkin, H. F. 1967. *The Concept of Representation*. Berkeley: University of California Press.

Plutzer, Eric, and Michael Berkman. 2005. The Graying of America and Support for Funding the Nation's Schools. *Public Opinion Quarterly* 69 (spring): 66–86.

Pommerehne, Werner W. 1978. Institutional Approaches to Public Expenditure: Empirical Evidence from Swiss Municipalities. *Journal of Public Economics* 9: 255–80.

Ponza, M., G. J. Duncan, M. Corcoran, and F. Groskind. 1988. The Guns of Autumn? Age Differences in Support for Income Transfers to the Young and Old. *Public Opinion Quarterly* 54, no. 4: 492–512.

Pool, Ithiel de Sola, Robert P. Abelson, and Samuel L. Popkin. 1965. *Candidates, Issues, and Strategies: A Computer Simulation of the 1960 and 1964 Presidential Elections*. Cambridge, Mass.: MIT Press.

Poterba, James M. 1997. Demographic Structure and the Political Economy of Public Education. *Journal of Policy Analysis and Management* 16, no. 1: 48–66.

———. 1998. Demographic Change, Intergenerational Linkages, and Public Education. *American Economic Association Papers and Proceedings* 88, no. 2: 315–20.

Preston, Samuel. 1984. Children and the Elderly in the United States. *Scientific American* 251 (December): 44–49.

Robinson, T. P., Robert E. England, and Kenneth J. Meier. 1985. Black Resources and

Black School-Board Representation: Does Political-Structure Matter? *Social Science Quarterly* 66, no. 4: 976–82.

Romer, Thomas, and Howard Rosenthal. 1982. Median Voters or Budget Maximizers: Evidence from School Expenditure Referenda. *Economic Inquiry* 20 (October): 556–78.

Romer, T., H. Rosenthal, and V. Munley. 1992. Economic Incentives and Political Institutions: Spending and Voting in School Budget Referenda. *Journal of Public Economics* 49, no. 1: 1–33.

Rose, Heather, and Jon Sonstelie. 2004. School Board Politics, School District Size and the Bargaining Power of Teachers' Unions. Unpublished manuscript, University of California, Santa Barbara.

Rosenbaum, Walter A., and James W. Button. 1989. Is There a Gray Peril? Retirement Politics in Florida. *Gerontologist* 29, no. 3: 300–6.

Rosenstone, Steven J., and John Mark Hansen. 1993. *Mobilization, Participation, and Democracy in America.* New York: Macmillan.

Salisbury, Robert H. 1980. *Citizen Participation in the Public Schools.* Lexington, Mass.: Lexington Books.

Saltzman, Gregory M. 1985. Bargaining Laws as a Cause and Consequence of the Growth of Teacher Unionism. *Industrial and Labor Relations Review* 38, no. 3: 335–51.

Scarrow, Howard. 1999. The Impact of At-large Elections: Vote Dilution or Choice Dilution? *Electoral Studies* 18, no. 4: 557–67.

Sears, David O., and Jack Citrin. 1982. *Tax Revolt: Something for Nothing.* Cambridge, Mass.: Harvard University Press.

Sears, David O., and Carolyn L. Funk. 1990. Self-Interest in Americans' Political Opinion. In *Beyond Self-Interest,* ed. J. J. Mansbridge. Chicago: University of Chicago Press.

Silva, Fabio, and Jon Sonstelie. 1995. Did Serrano Cause a Decline in School Spending? *National Tax Journal* 48, no. 2: 199–215.

Sirkin, J. R. 1985. Experts Predict Struggle Ahead to Maintain Education Funding. *Education Week,* April 24. http://www.edweek.org.

Skowronek, Stephen. 1982. *Building a New American State: The Expansion of National Administrative Capacities.* Cambridge: Cambridge University Press.

South, Scott J. 1991. Age Structure and Public Expenditures on Children. *Social Science Quarterly* 72, no. 4: 661–75.

Steunenberg, Bernard. 1992. Referendum, Initiative, and Veto Power: Budgetary Decision Making in Local Government. *Kyklos* 4, no.4: 501–29.

Stevens, Joe B., and Robert Mason. 1996. Political Markets, Property Tax Referenda, and Local School Funding. *Public Choice* 86: 257–77.

Stewart, Joseph Jr., Robert E. England, and Kenneth J. Meier. 1989. Black Representation in Urban School Districts: From School Board to Office to Classroom. *Western Political Quarterly* 42, no. 2: 287–305.

Strang, D. 1987. The Administrative Transformation of American Education: School District Consolidation 1938–1980. *Administrative Science Quarterly* 32: 352–66.

Strate, John M., Charles M. Parrish, Charles D. Elder, and Coit Ford III. 1989. Life Span Civic Development and Voting Participation. *American Political Science Review* 83, no. 2: 443–64.

Swain, Carol. 1995. *Black Faces, Black Interests: The Representation of African Americans in Congress.* Cambridge, Mass.: Harvard University Press.

Taylor, Steven. 2001. Appointing or Electing the Boston School Committee: The Preferences of the African American Community. *Urban Education* 36, no. 1:4–26.

Tedin, Kent L. 1994. Self-Interest and Symbolic Politics in the Financial Equalization of the Public Schools. *Journal of Politics* 56, no. 3: 628–49.

Tedin, Kent L., Richard E. Matland, and Gregory R. Weiher. 2001. Age, Race, Self-Interest and Financing Public Schools through Referenda. *Journal of Politics* 63, no. 1: 270–94.

Tiebout, Charles M. 1956. A Pure Theory of Local Expenditures. *Journal of Political Economy* 64 , no. 5: 416–24.

Toland, Bill. 2005. Rendell Criticizes School Boards. *Pittsburgh Post-Gazette,* June 1, 2005.

Turnbull, Geoffrey K., and Peter M. Mitias. 1999. The Median Voter Model across Levels of Government. *Public Choice* 99: 119–38.

Tyack, David B. 1974. *The One Best System: A History of American Urban Education.* Cambridge, Mass.: Harvard University Press.

Tyack, David B., and Larry Cuban. 1995. *Tinkering toward Utopia: A Century of Public School Reform.* Cambridge, Mass.: Harvard University Press.

U.S. Bureau of the Census. 1995. Annual Housing Vacancy Survey, Table 15. http://www. census.gov/hhes/www/housing/hvs/annual95/ann95t15.html.

Vinovskis, Maris A. 1993. A Historical Perspective on Support for Schooling by Different Age Cohorts. In *The Changing Contract across Generations,* ed. Vern L. Benston and W. Andrew Achenbaum. New York: Aldine De Gruyter.

Weber, Ronald E., Anne H. Hopkins, Michael L. Mezey, and Frank J. Munger. 1972. Computer Simulation of State Electorates. *Public Opinion Quarterly* 36, no. 4: 549–65.

Weber, Ronald E., and William R. Shaffer. 1972. Public Opinion and American State Policy-Making. *Midwest Journal of Political Science* 16, no. 4: 683–99.

Weimer, David L., and Michael J. Wolkoff. 2001. School Performance and Housing Values: Using Non-Contiguous District and Incorporation Boundaries to Identify School Effects. *National Tax Journal* 54, no. 3: 231–53.

Weingast, Barry, Kenneth A. Shepsle, and Christopher Johnsen. 1981. The Political Economy of Benefits and Costs: A Neoclassical Approach to Distributive Politics. *Journal of Political Economy* 89, no. 4: 642–64.

Welch, Susan. 1990. The Impact of At-large Elections on the Representation of Blacks and Hispanics. *Journal of Politics* 52, no. 4: 1050–76.

Welch, Susan, and Timothy Bledsoe. 1988. *Urban Reform and Its Consequences: A Study in Representation.* Chicago: University of Chicago Press.

Welch, Susan, and Albert Karnig. 1978. Representation of Blacks on Big City School Boards. *Social Science Quarterly* 59, no. 1: 162–72.

Werner, B. L. 1998. Urbanization, Proximity, and the Intra-State Context of Women's Representation. *Women & Politics* 19, no. 2: 81–93.

Wheeler, Ginger. 2000. Referendum Gamesmanship: Strategies for Winning Over the Skeptics in Your Community. *American School Board Journal,* January, 46–47.

Wirt, Frederick M., and Michael W. Kirst. 1997. *The Political Dynamics of American Education.* Berkeley, Calif.: McCutchan.

Wolfinger, Raymond, and Steven J. Rosenstone. 1980. *Who Votes?* New Haven, Conn.: Yale University Press.

Wong, Kenneth. 1991. State Reform in Education Finance: Territorial and Social Strategies. *Publius: The Journal of Federalism* 21, no. 3: 125–42.

———. 1995. The Politics of Education: From Political Science to Multidisciplinary Inquiry. In *The Study of Educational Politics: The 1994 Commemorative Yearbook of the Politics of Education Association,* ed. Jay D. Scribner and Donald H. Layton. Washington, D.C.: Falmer Press.

———. 1999. *Funding Public Schools: Politics and Policies.* Lawrence: University of Kansas Press.

Zax, Jeffrey S. 1989a. Initiatives and Government Expenditures. *Public Choice* 63: 267–77.

Zax, Jeffrey, and Casey Ichniowski. 1988. The Effects of Public Sector Unionism on Pay, Employment, Department Budgets, and Municipal Expenditures. In *When Public Sector Workers Organize,* ed. Richard B. Freeman and Casey Ichniowski. Chicago: University of Chicago Press.

Zodrow, George R. 2001. Reflections on the New View and the Benefit View of the Property Tax. In *Property Taxation and Local Government Finance,* ed. Wallace E Oates. Cambridge, Mass.: Lincoln Institute of Land Policy.

Index

racial/ethnic differences as factors in, 41–43, 51

social cleavages and the demographic sources of, 36–48, 50–52, 61, 149–50

socioeconomic status as a factor in, 44–46

spending preferences by state and, 54–62

state contexts and the methodology of modeling, 49–52

study of at district level, small polity inference approach to (*see* small polity inference)

study of at district level, traditional approaches to, 52–53, 59, 161–65

race

appointed school boards and, 102–6

descriptive representation and policy responsiveness, 100–102, 108–9

discriminatory elections, the quiet revolution against, 88–94

elected school boards and, 107–8

electoral system reform and, 86–88

minority representation after electoral reform, 95–100

residential segregation, 109–10

support for educational spending and, 41–43

See also African Americans

random coefficients model. *See* hierarchical linear model

referendum, the

bond referenda, 69, 83n.8

the initiative, distinguished from, 73

in Pennsylvania, 154–56

policy responsiveness and, 72–77, 80–82

school funding, requirements for, 69–71

town meeting, distinguished from, 71

Rendell, Edward, 151–52, 156

representation, descriptive and substantive, 87–88. *See also* descriptive representation; substantive representation

residential segregation, 109–10

Rhode Island, 78

Rodriguez v. San Antonio School District, 33n.2

Rohrer, Charles, 155

Romer, Thomas, 83n.12

Rosenthal, H., 83n.12

Rubinfield, Daniel L., 42

Sallack, David, 159n.6

school boards

appointed, policy responsiveness of, 102–6

citizen preferences and policies of, correspondence between (*see* policy responsiveness)

democratic governance and, xvii–xviii, 2–4

directors and members, number of, 12

elected, policy responsiveness of, 106–8

elections for (*see* elections/electoral systems)

minority representation on, 95–100

Progressive Era reforms, impact of, 3–4, 147

variation in, 1–2, 15

school districts

citizen budget power in (*see* citizen budget power)

consolidation of, 18–21

the elderly in (*see* elderly citizens)

evolution of, 18–25

funding of (*see* financing education)

homogeneity of, 149

independent promoted by Progressives, 63–65

independent vs. dependent, financial responsibilities of, 26

independent vs. dependent, policy responsiveness of, 63–68

as laboratories of governance, 158

per-pupil expenditures as basis for comparison across, 29–31

public opinion in (*see* public opinion; small polity inference)

selection of school boards (*see* elections/electoral systems; school boards)

state governments and, 17–18 (*see also* state governments)

teachers' unions and (*see* teachers' unions)

Schwab, Robert, 34n.9

Serano v. Priest, 19–21, 27

Shah, Mona P., 33n.9

Shapiro, Perry, 42

Silva, Fabio, 34n.9

simulation approach to opinion estimation, 52–53, 59, 162–64

Skowronek, Stephen, 146